More Testimonials

"This tremendously insightful book tells how to use amazing techniques to unleash the power of the subconscious and to put it to work in your personal and professional life."

—Paul J. Meyer, Chairman,
Success Motivation Institute, Inc.

"Your ideas are super. I believe, support, and practice your philosophy. Your message applies equally to sales, manufacturing, technical, financial, research, and all areas of business. All have to sell themselves and their ideas or projects to succeed."

—Clyde H. Boyd, Former President,
Dow Chemical, Europe

"I genuinely believe your book will receive great public acceptance. I'm looking forward to purchasing one of the first copies off the press."

—Rex L. Davis, JD, CPCU, CLU,
Chairman, United Republic Reinsurance Company

"I could not read your manuscript fast enough. There are a certain number of books I feel are must reading for the new salesman. Dale Carnegie's, *How To Win Friends and Influence People*, is one of them. In all honesty, I believe yours will take first place. You have a winner. Probably the most prevalent thing in the manuscript was the ability to place myself in the sales situations you used as examples. Did you write this using me as the test case?"

—Don Kitzmiller, Vice President, Marketing/Sales,
Midmark

"Your focus on practical application of the subconscious mind is excellent. Please send me an early copy of what I expect to be millions. Good Luck!"

—John C. Kalenberg, President,
Carlson Learning Company

THE
SECRETS
OF
SUPERSELLING

*How to Program
Your Subconscious
for Success*

BY
Lynéa Corson, Ph.D.,
George Hadley, Ed.D.,
Carl Stevens, CPAE

BERKLEY BOOKS, NEW YORK

Dedicated to our many clients
from whom we have learned so much
and without whom this could never have been written.

THE SECRETS OF SUPERSELLING

A Berkley Book / published by arrangement with
the authors

PRINTING HISTORY
Berkley trade paperback edition / April 1991

ISBN: 0-425-12661-7

A BERKLEY BOOK ® TM 757,375
Berkley Books are published by The Berkley Publishing Group,
200 Madison Avenue, New York, New York 10016.
The name "BERKLEY" and the "B" logo
are trademarks belonging to Berkley Publishing Corporation.

PRINTED IN THE UNITED STATES OF AMERICA

10 9 8 7 6 5 4 3 2 1

CONTENTS

INTRODUCTION: WHAT THE SECRETS OF SUPERSELLING CAN DO FOR YOU

Chrysler's Lee Iacocca believes that sales technique is the key to advancement for anyone in business.

Thomas Watson, Jr., former CEO of IBM said the key to the company's growth was not being the first in a given technology, but in knowing how to sell it.

The American Management Association conducted a survey, asking, "What single, personal proficiency will most determine your entire level of achievement throughout life?" Two thousand eight hundred top business leaders replied, "Your ability to sell yourself and your ideas."

The *National Sales Executives Digest* surveyed several thousand salespeople in an attempt to discover their most secret thoughts, feelings, and frustrations about their careers in selling. Two of their three most frequently stated needs were: specific methods for improving sales . . . not **what** to do, but **how** to do it; and training in digest form that is readable, educational, short, explanatory, illustrated with actual case histories, and believable.

A Prentice Hall, Inc. survey of 4,000 salespeople illustrates the enormous need for *how-to* information. These salespeople reported that only 10 percent of their efforts earned money for them; 90 percent of the work they did was worthless.

According to *Harvard Business Review*, the selection and training of field sales managers has become one of the most acute problems facing top management. Over half the sales managers surveyed had never read a job description of what they were supposed to do. Seventy-eight percent of the same sales managers were either dissatisfied with their training or had never received any specific training to equip them for their roles as sales managers.

The Secrets of SuperSelling answers all these needs. It consists of educational material written in simple language, along with step-by-step instructions on how to apply the information. It teaches you how to use the almost limitless potential of your brain and subconscious mind to sell yourself, your ideas, and your product.

Think and Grow Rich by Napoleon Hill is a classic based on Hill's twenty-year study of very successful people. When he examined high achievers, he found that there were some who accomplished their results with an ease and speed that was amazing. *The Secrets of SuperSelling* came about from an in-depth look at similar high achievers to determine *how* they were achieving their results so quickly and easily.

Many of these high achievers instinctively utilized methods and principles unknown to many people. We found, however, that what they did instinctively could be documented, learned, and put into practice by anyone willing to follow the step-by-step methods outlined in our Secrets. The authors have gleaned these field-tested methods from their 110 combined years of study and hands-on experience with thousands of executives and salespeople in the United States and other countries.

This information is not meant to replace the fine sales or management training you have received from your company, or learned on your own. Instead, it provides you with an easy-to-follow method of tapping into your personal power, so that you utilize your training to a much higher level, and tap into even more of your potential.

The Secrets of SuperSelling is unique in that it supplies the missing link—the How To Do It—of harnessing your subconscious mind and creating your Positive Magnetic Energy Field. Previously published materials fail to mention the importance of developing a magnetic energy field to help you achieve goals with an ease that seems magical. They also fail to tell you how to control and direct your subconscious. The importance of controlling your mind is validated by W. Clement Stone, founder of *Success* magazine who says, "Most sales are made because of the way the salesman, not the prospect, thinks and acts."

The Secrets of SuperSelling presents an exciting new way to increase sales utilizing methods and strategies founded upon the latest social, psychological, and scientific research. It teaches you the following:

1. How to Identify What Is Programmed Into Your Subconscious Mind
2. How to Dissolve Programming You No Longer Want
3. How to Program Your Subconscious for Quicker and Easier Results
4. How to Harness Your Physical, Emotional, and Mental Energy to Work Smarter, Not Harder
5. How to Create Your Positive Magnetic Energy Field

The Secrets you are about to learn are presently used by business owners, executives, and salespeople throughout the United States and a number of foreign countries. They have never failed anyone who has used them as presented. They are easy to learn, and exciting to use. When properly applied, they can keep you from repeating unproductive experiences and show you how to achieve results you may have only dreamed of. As you continue to be successful over a long period of time, you will be delighted with these new-found tools, and the power they give you.

Here are a few examples of people who have successfully used *The Secrets of SuperSelling*.

- Henry L. was twenty-ninth in sales out of 800 agents in his company. In one year's time, he doubled his income, moved up to thirteenth, and worked less hours.
- Betty R., vice president of marketing in a major bank in the East, created a new way to market the bank's products which no other banks were using.
- Bruce W. tripled his income in nine months and made the largest sale in his office's history.

You may be thinking, "Can this really be true? Is it possible that by simply applying these secrets I can double my income while working less hours, or make the largest sale ever made in my office's or business's history? I bet these secrets have something to do with positive thinking, and you're going to tell me that affirmations and visualizations can increase my sales. *That's all very interesting, but what about the realities of selling?"*

THE TRUTH ABOUT REALITY

Scientists have proven in laboratory studies that the mind of a human being can affect inert material. In the authors' own personal investigations, it has been proven over and over that the preconceived reality of a line of sales or a business can be affected or changed by the power of the mind.

In real estate, for example, many believe that it takes from three to six months to make the first sale. In insurance, many believe that they must work for five years before they make any "real" money. There are statistics for how many phone calls you need to make to reach a certain number of people. . . . how many people you need to see to close a certain amount of sales. . . . how many salespeople you need to sell X amount of product, and how long it takes to get a certain amount of work done. Statistics are certainly a necessary part of our world. However, we have found that these generally-believed statistics about selling can be changed. By applying *The Secrets of Super-Selling*, you can create your own reality just the way you'd like it to be.

Example: Bill is a mortgage loan originator. His experiences with real estate transactions led him to believe that all real estate deals have problems. For example, his deals with some agents frequently involved crises at the end which were eventually solved, and the deals then closed. Other agents often challenged his creativity, for the majority of their clients presented severe financial problems.

After attending a Secrets workshop, and learning that you can create your own reality the way you'd like it to be, Bill decided to try an experiment. He and a real estate agent who had also attended the workshop set a goal to see just how many deals they could create in a row that had absolutely no hitches in them! The startling news is that with this new belief that real estate deals need not have hitches, they put together thirty-four transactions in a row that went through as smooth as glass!

The truth about reality is that you are already creating your *own* reality by programming your subconscious mind, and creating a magnetic energy field that is constantly affecting your achievement. The exciting news is that by applying these Secrets, you can learn to control your subconscious mind, have your conscious and subconscious work in concert for you, and create a positive magnetic energy field to get what you want quicker and easier.

SELLING YOURSELF, YOUR IDEAS AND YOUR PRODUCT

The Secrets of SuperSelling details a dynamic means of displacing limitations programmed into your subconscious that keep you from reaching your ultimate potential. This "how-to" approach helps you to displace "the old," reprogram your subconscious mind, and replace limiting ideas with "the new" . . . thereby achieving what you want.

The Secrets of SuperSelling is much more than a simple process of positive thinking, or the use of affirmations and visualizations. It is a synthesis of work from education, quantum physics, metaphysics, sales training, and psychotherapy. Its purpose is to put you in the driver's seat of one of the most powerful creative instruments known to mankind . . . your **subconscious mind.** The principles and techniques presented here have been scientifically documented. They are structured to allow you to progressively acquire the success habits of the highest achievers. Follow the Secret-by-Secret instructions, master the techniques presented, and you will progressively use more and more of your potential to achieve your dreams.

The Secrets of SuperSelling involves more than just writing Positive Denial Statements and Affirmations, and visualizing what you want. Each Secret is an integral part of the puzzle. Unless you have every piece, you do not have the full picture. You must identify in specific terms what it is you want. You must use both left-brain and right-brain thinking styles to program your subconscious mind. You must create a positive magnetic energy field to draw to you the things you want. You must update your self image so that you can keep what you get. You must celebrate your successes to motivate yourself and to increase the power of your energy field. You must take inventory of your subconscious just as you would take inventory in a store to see what is there. You must clear out beliefs, attitudes, and feelings that limit your achievement. You must take time to feed your mind on a daily basis just as you take time to feed your body.

The Secrets of SuperSelling has been designed for learning, not entertainment. The fun comes from achieving the results you create through applying the principles. Select a regular time when your mind can be still, a time for concentrated learning. Read and internalize the ideas and techniques. For optimal results, take the time to do the activities at the end of each Secret.

Don't let your mind discount any of the information presented. Don't rename the process as "just doing affirmations" or "just having a positive mental attitude." Don't devalue your reasons for wanting to achieve even greater success. Don't decide that this information isn't going to help you because you have already read books or even attended workshops. Don't discount the effect self-improvement has on sales. Above all, don't procrastinate— put these ideas into practice.

You'll be limiting yourself if you read just a few pages, get some good results, then put the book aside. Richard is an insurance agent who usually closed three out of five prospects. However, for eight months he had not been getting sales. He read the first Secret and sold $7,000 in premiums in one week and closed three out of three. He then read sixty-two more pages, and earned $4,200 profit. He called one of the authors and excitedly reported, "As soon as I applied the Secrets, things started popping!"

The process of programming your subconscious is the same for selling yourself, your ideas, or your product. You see the successful outcome before you start the physical actions needed to achieve the goal. You apply all the Secrets to the goal whether it be selling yourself in a job interview or selling yourself on doing what is needed to accomplish your goal . . . selling your ideas to your sales force or selling your product to your prospect.

So what are you waiting for? This is your golden opportunity to achieve your own personal and professional dreams. You can get started right away by completing the "Dream List" described below. Let your mind wander. Don't censor your thoughts. Write down every desire that comes to you. Then turn to Secret One and begin one of the most exciting and rewarding experiences of your life.

We thank you for the opportunity to share these Secrets with you. Our mutual mission is to help you gain control of your subconscious mind so that you make more sales, earn more money, and have more fun doing it!

DREAM LIST

Directions: Let your mind wander. Don't judge your desires. On a separate sheet of paper, write down everything you'd like to be, do, or have. You will use this information throughout the Secrets. Add to this list as often as you wish.

THE
SECRETS
OF
SUPERSELLING

Secret One

Understand How Your Subconscious Works

PREVIEW OF SECRET ONE

UNDERSTAND HOW YOUR SUBCONSCIOUS WORKS

Just as it is important to be computer-literate in today's world, it is equally important that you become brain-literate. Secret One brings you the latest findings on how your brain works, as well as the fourteen principles governing your subconscious. You'll discover how your subconscious helps create your reality; that you have no choice in whether to use it or not; and that it cannot reject whatever is programmed into it. As your obedient servant, your subconscious works day and night to obtain both your consciously and unconsiously created sales and management goals, as well as your goals in all other areas of your life. Your subconscious is the key to getting what you want in life, so it is important that you take charge of its programming. The exciting news is that you *do* have a choice in what you create with this wonderful genie in the bottle.

UNDERSTAND HOW YOUR SUBCONSCIOUS WORKS

MEET YOUR SUBCONSCIOUS

The subconscious was first discovered in the eighteenth century by Anton Mesmer, an Austrian physician and hypnotist. Sigmund Freud, the father of psychoanalysis, later explored it, and wrote extensively about this phenomenon.

Maxwell Maltz wrote in his book, *Psycho-Cybernetics*, that what is often called the subconscious mind is actually not a mind at all. It is a wonderful, goal-striving mechanism made up of the brain and nervous system. The goals that it seeks to achieve are the mental images you have created in your imagination.

Anything you do or get is first created within your mind. There are numerous accounts in printed literature of people actually achieving results through mental processes alone. One such account appeared in the *Reader's Digest* in April 1955. It was a story of how Alekhine beat the great chess champion, Capablanca, who was considered unbeatable because he was so superior at the game.

Three months before the match, Alekhine retired to the country. He stopped smoking and drinking, and exercised a great deal. The startling part of this story is that during that time, he played chess only in his imagination, yet beat the "unbeatable" Capablanca!

The power of the mind is further illustrated in an experiment conducted using athletes. A group of basketball players shot a

certain number of free-throws, and their average score of baskets made was recorded. The players were then divided into
three groups. Group One was asked to refrain from practicing for
thirty days. Group Two was asked to practice free-throws for one
hour a day for thirty days. Group Three was asked to practice the
same length of time, but only in their imagination. They were to
picture themselves stepping up to the free-throw line and tossing
the ball through the hoop each time.

At the end of thirty days, the three groups were again tested
for free-throw accuracy. As you might expect, Group One made
no improvement. Group Two, which had practiced each day,
made a twenty-four percent gain in average baskets. Ironically,
Group Three, which also practiced each day, but only through
imagination, made a twenty-three percent gain.

The results of this and similar experiments have led many
coaches and athletes to include visualization as part of their
regular training program.

THE MOST POWERFUL, CREATIVE INSTRUMENT IN THE UNIVERSE

Your subconscious never sleeps and cannot be idle. It is actively
engaged at all times in seeking to achieve goals you have created
in your imagination. If there is something you really want, your
subconscious has no choice but to get it for you.

Along with creating positive conditions, your subconscious can
just as easily create negative ones. If you worry about a problem,
and dream up all kinds of dire consequences, your subconscious
has no choice but to create them.

If you accidentally create negative conditions and realize it,
your subconscious has the power to turn those conditions around
in a very short period of time. It can heal your body, or end a
selling slump. As you tell yourself that you are well and totally
healthy, or that you continually make sales, your subconscious
makes literal truth out of the positive statements, just as it made
literal truth out of your former fears.

Hypnosis is a good example of how your subconscious makes

literal truth out of suggestions. A subject is placed under hypnosis, and a bottle of ammonia is passed under his nose. He is told that he is smelling a bouquet of roses. As he takes a big sniff, a smile comes over his face. When he is no longer hypnotized, smelling the same bottle of ammonia brings tears to his eyes. The subject's subconscious made literal truth out of the hypnotist's statements, just as your subconscious makes literal truth out of your thoughts and feelings.

Your Subconscious is Your Obedient Servant

- Your subconscious steers you in the right direction to achieve your goals. It helps you be in the right place at the right time, saying and doing the right things.
- It works night and day to find solutions to your problems.
- It provides new ideas or inspiration for you.

Your subconscious is your obedient servant, and follows any blueprint provided. Understanding the following principles and developing your own blueprints puts you in the driver's seat of one of the most powerful sales tools that exists!

PRINCIPLES OF YOUR SUBCONSCIOUS

Principle Number One: Your Subconscious Needs Precise Goals

Your subconscious seeks to achieve goals that are mental images you have created in your imagination. In creating these mental images, you need to make clear-cut decisions about precise amounts and specific characteristics.

If you wish to program your subconscious to reach a goal such as being good in sales, you need to give it precise instructions such as the following: "I sell owners of companies who have twenty-five or more employees. I service the customers well, and get repeat business over and over for as long as I am in sales. I am in the top ten percent of the salespeople in our company." This assures you of getting *exactly* what you want with ease and speed.

Because your subconscious works so efficiently to get you what you say you want, you must be careful in the wording of your goals. If you look at your present income of $25,000 and decide you want to earn $35,000 in the next twelve months, your subconscious will do what is needed to produce that amount of income. However, if you say, "I am going to make more money in the next twelve months than I did last year," you may earn only $25,050. Without clearly specified targets, your subconscious takes the accumulated decisions you have made in the past regarding income, along with your actual past income, and produces a result based on the law of averages. You then get an average of your past earnings.

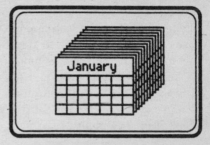

Principle Number Two: Your Subconscious Takes You Literally

Confucius was once asked what his first deed would be if he were to be made Emperor of China. He replied, "I would re-establish the precise meaning of words." Let's look at how the words you think and say can affect your sales.

You are a commissioned salesperson selling a product. You contact people on the telephone, and set appointments to meet with them. It is a new month, and you have a quota to meet.

You think, "Wow, I have got to get on the phone and make calls!"

You are on the phone all day. You talk to thirty-two prospects, but don't set one appointment. In addition, you make twenty-eight more calls and reach secretaries or family members of prospects. You feel like the day was wasted and you failed.

You did not fail. You were successful with the goal you set which was to get on the phone and make calls.

It's not enough to say you need to make some calls or even to say you need to set some appointments. Your goal is not to make calls or set appointments.

Your goal is to make sales.

Example: Here is an example of how to word your goals to produce the results you want. You decide, "I have to get on the phone and set some good appointments to make sales. I have to close enough prospects to deposit at least $5,000 in my bank account by the end of this month."

You get on the phone and reach nineteen people in two-and-a-half hours. You set appointments with twelve of them. You sell all but two. You deposit a little more than $5,000 in your bank account for the month.

Your subconscious takes you literally, and works to give you exactly what you say.

Principle Number Three: Your Subconscious Needs Upgraded Goals on a Regular Basis

While your subconscious needs precise goals on which to work, it is also necessary to upgrade your goals on a regular basis. Neglecting to do this results in commissioned sales people earning about the same amount of money month after month, year after year. Their paychecks look like they're salaried. The following example illustrates this point.

Example: A salesman set a goal to make eight sales a month. He wrote out the projected income and sales for the coming year.

Since he was new in sales, he believed the goal to make eight sales each month was an ambitious one.

The first three months in the business, he barely met his goals. The fourth month, he reached his goal of eight sales in the first week. Everyone he called on after that told him to call back in a few weeks because of time pressures, money, and so on. This continued until the end of the month. The first week of the next month, he started making sales again.

If he had realized the power of his subconscious to stop sales once he had reached his declared goal, he could have immediately reset it for a higher amount. This would have allowed him to continue selling after he had reached his declared monthly goal during the first week.

Your subconscious doesn't upgrade your goals on its own. You must do this yourself. By keeping written records of stated goals, dates for their achievement, and your income, you can upgrade your goals when you find you are achieving them faster than you anticipated. This will protect you from having a great run of sales in a short period of time, and no sales for a long time after that.

STEPS FOR UPGRADING YOUR GOALS.

1. Keep written records of what you have sold on a monthly basis, as well as the yearly income goal you have set, so you can increase your yearly goal when you are ahead of schedule on a monthly basis.
2. Raise your yearly income goal after having an unusually big month or sale.
3. When you set a specific production goal that is a little higher than the month before, be sure to raise your yearly income goal, also.

Principle Number Four: Once an Idea is Accepted by Your Subconscious, You Will Continue to Have That Result in Your Life

When your subconscious has accepted an idea, nothing can stop you from realizing the results of that idea except your dissolving it from your subconscious.

- If you hold on to the idea that your closing average is one out of seven, your closing average will stay at one out of seven. If you hold on to the idea that your closing average is now one out of two it will stay at one out of two.
- If you think it is impossible to find a better way to market your product, you will continue to market your product the same way.

Your subconscious continues to create the same result over and over until you tell it to stop.

Example: In *Psycho-Cybernetics*, Maxwell Maltz tells of a man who was a top producer for his company. Because of this, his employers gave him a better territory. However, much to their disappointment, he continued to produce the same amount of sales. He was later given a "not-so-good" territory. To their amazement, he still produced the same amount of sales.

This man's experience shows that reaching your goal is not solely dependent on the territory, the economy, the product, etc. The critical factor is what you have programmed into your subconscious.

Principle Number Five: When an Idea Is Dissolved From Your Subconscious, You No Longer Have That Result in Your Life

You can learn to dissolve any idea that you no longer want from your subconscious. When you dissolve the idea that there is no better way to market your product, you open your mind to discovering new marketing methods. When you dissolve the idea that your closing average is one out of seven, you will be able to choose and obtain a higher closing average.

 Freedom comes from dissolving the idea from your subconscious by repeatedly affirming, "My closing average is no longer one out of seven, it is now one out of two." Through repetition, your subconscious accepts this new idea, then finds ways for you to improve your closing average.

Principle Number Six: Your Subconscious Acts on Your Most Dominant Thought

Your subconscious acts on your most dominant thought. It has a perfect memory for everything you have ever experienced, right down to the smallest details, and remembers all the decisions you have ever made.

You may have decided as a young child, "I want to be a salesperson. I know I'd be a good salesperson." Now as an adult, you may doubt your ability to do well in sales. Your subconscious is going to produce results for you based on the thought you believe most. This accounts for your selling like a dynamo one month when you believed your childhood decision, and not selling very much another month, when you believed the doubt you created as an adult.

Let's look at another example of conflicting thoughts. In the real estate profession, prospects choose properties and make offers. Many details must be handled between the offers and final ownership of the properties. There are times when deals appear destined to fall apart. Agents work diligently to keep them together by smoothing ruffled feathers and handling unexpected emergencies.

Sometimes the contracts get salvaged and troublesome deals go through; sometimes they don't. There are many people adding their mental, physical, and emotional energies to the situation. If everyone involved believes the deals are going to go through easily with no hitches, they very often do.

However, if those involved in the transaction get caught up in ambivalent feelings and thoughts, the subconscious will always act on the most dominant thought. . . . the one with the most power and conviction. When there is a strong desire for the house to sell, and also a strong fear that it won't because houses aren't selling very well at this time, the result will depend on which thoughts and feelings are dominant. Remember, if your dominant thought is that this sale is going through no matter what, and your feelings are those of confidence and determination, you will make the sale.

Principle Number Seven: Your Subconscious Needs Repetition

Planting an idea in your subconscious is similar to planting seeds in the ground. If you plant seeds in your garden, then walk away and never fertilize and water them, you probably will not reap a harvest. However, if you plant the seeds, then lovingly tend them day after day, you will probably get a good harvest. The same holds true for your mind. If you think a thought only once or twice, you probably won't get the result you desired. It would be like casually dropping seeds in the ground. . . . walking away from them. . . . and expecting them to grow.

The findings of Professor Hermann Ebbinghaus, Educational Psychologist, validates the power of repetition of thought. He found that if you hear something only once, four days later you will have forgotten 85% of what you heard. In sixteen days you will have forgotten 98% of the material. However, if you hear the same information six to eight times in a week, thirty days later, you will remember 90% or more of what you heard.

Based on this research, you see that if you give yourself a new suggestion, it will fade away if not repeated. If you have had a fear of cold calls, and write the statement, "I'm not afraid to make cold calls," it will not change your behavior unless you read it on a daily basis over a period of time. The old suggestion, "I'm afraid to make cold calls," is firmly planted in your subconscious, and it will come bouncing back. You must dissolve the old suggestion, "I'm afraid to make cold calls" and repeat the new one, "I'm great on cold calls" until the new one becomes firmly planted in your subconscious.

Principle Number Eight: Time Means Nothing to Your Subconscious

Time means nothing to your subconscious. It has no sense of past, present, or future. Everything is now. This means you can make your sales quota in the last few days of the month if you need to do so. It is not carved in stone that it takes two weeks to close that many deals. You are the one who puts that idea into your subconscious.

One day?
One week?
One month?
One year?
It's up to you!

The choice is yours. Your subconscious can produce results very quickly and easily if you allow it to do so. However, you can't force your subconscious into action by pushing and struggling. Instead, you allow it to produce results. There is no set amount of time needed. The amount of time is determined by what you truly believe is possible and how intensely you desire the result.

Principle Number Nine: What You Believe Determines What You See in Your Imagination

Your subconscious takes you literally and produces results based on your beliefs. If you have a problem and think there is a solution, but believe on a feeling level there is no way to solve it, you will keep the problem. To believe means to have confidence in, to trust, or to come to expect. In this case, your belief is stronger than your thought, which results in an image being created in your brain of not solving the problem. As you look at this internal picture over and over, you feel even more upset about it. This programs your subconscious to intensify the problem.

As a manager, you may have a goal to increase sales by thirty percent. When you're around your superiors and everyone is enthusiastic about reaching the objective, you may feel sure of reaching it. However, once you're back in your office going over daily reports, you see that absenteeism is high. You start doubting your ability to lead your group in such a way that you achieve your company's objective.

If you see-saw back and forth between belief that you'll reach your objective and fear that you won't, your group's production will fluctuate depending on which belief is strongest at the moment.

Once you are definite in your belief that you will meet the goal of increased sales, people who produce little will either change their production, or suddenly leave your company. Those leaving will be replaced by staff who have good attendance, a desire to work, and a feeling of satisfaction in helping the company reach it's goals.

Principle Number Ten: What You See Is What You Get

You are probably familiar with the saying, "A picture is worth a thousand words." You may also remember Flip Wilson, the TV star, who made a comedy routine around, "What you see is what you get." Both statements are true of your subconscious.

For your subconscious to achieve your goal, it must get the *picture* of what you want. You must also see yourself as being successful before you actually reach your goal. This is covered more fully in Secret Six, Realize The Power Of Your Self-Image.

Principle Number Eleven: Previous Experiences Are Repeated

When your subconscious is given a task to accomplish, it searches through past experiences to find similar ones and repeats them.

In *Psycho-Cybernetics*, Maxwell Maltz reported on the work of Dr. John C. Eccles and Sir Charles Sherrington, experts in the field of brain physiology. They wrote that the cortex of the human brain is composed of ten billion neurons, each having many axons with synapses or connections between the neurons. Electrical impulses run along these neurons and must bridge the gap between the synapses. If you can imagine a tree with many branches standing next to a similar tree, you have a good picture of the brain's neurons. The space between the branches of the trees are the synapses, or connecting points. Now imagine a squirrel running up the tree, jumping across to the other tree, and running through those branches.

This gives you a picture of the electrical energy in your brain running along a pathway and bridging the gap as it continues to its destination. For every successful action you have ever performed in the past, you have a tattooing effect on your brain (a branch on the tree).

For example, if you have made several sales in a row, you have the tattooing effect on your brain of selling successfully. As you continue to make sales, the tattooing effect (pathways) become stronger. Interestingly enough, it doesn't make any difference whether you actually make the sales, or just imagine yourself making them. Your mind can't tell the difference between what you really do and what you picture in your mind. You can produce the tattooing effect on your brain through picturing the sales in your imagination, just as you can through actually making the sales. As mentioned in the beginning of this Secret, athletes have made excellent use of this principle for years through experiencing desired results in their imaginations in addition to their actual, daily practice.

Principle Number Twelve: Incubation Time Is Needed for Problem-Solving and Goal Achievement

Books on creativity state that many people find the answers to problems and new inventions in hunches and dreams. These people find that if they do extensive fact gathering and conscious thinking, then relax and take a nap or do some routine task which requires very little concentration, the insights and hunches which lead to discoveries then pop into their minds. Einstein used this process to his advantage: it is reported that he took naps when stumped by problems. He got his conscious mind out of the way which allowed his subconscious to synthesize and create.

When you give your subconscious a problem to solve and a deadline for its solution, it goes back through all the stored information and former experiences to select pertinent data. It then synthesizes this information. Next, it looks at the whole picture and discovers the missing detail or locates the right procedure to achieve your result. It then delivers a solution while you are doing something that doesn't require concentration.

During the incubation time, your right brain is working diligently on your problem, just as your left brain has been doing. The difference is that you are conscious of your left-brain thoughts and ideas. You frequently are not consciously aware of the activity of your right brain. It may seem as if you are not working on the task. This is not so. However, for your right brain to do its job, your left brain must relinquish control . . . pass it on to the next department, so to speak.

Relaxation is a key factor here. Stop worrying and trying to "figure it out." Do something that is relaxing to you. Be in a state of calm expectancy. Give your brain permission to interrupt you when it has completed the task and has an answer for you. Then, while you're doing something that doesn't require too much active concentration, the answer will suddenly pop into your awareness.

Principle Thirteen: Your Subconscious Needs Feeling Energy

As you learned in Principle Seven, repetition of your desired result is necessary for your subconscious to accept your goal. Along with repetition, it is crucial that you generate strong feelings about your goal. These can be feelings of excitement, joy, relief, desire, pride, determination, etc. The more intensely you experience your feelings about your goal, the easier it is for your subconscious to produce the result.

Do not single out any one principle and think you can achieve the results you want by applying only that one. All principles must be understood and applied to enjoy the full benefits from your powerful subconscious.
In subsequent Secrets, you will learn how to apply the principles to help you sell yourself, your ideas, and your product.

GETTING ACQUAINTED WITH YOUR BRAIN

A major factor in programming your subconscious is being able to use your whole brain effectively, knowing how your right and left brain function, and understanding some basic information about your brain in general.

Over the last two decades, research into the function of the human brain has given us a much clearer idea of how it operates. Studies of the brain are at the frontiers of science, and these exciting discoveries are now reaching the general public.

Research has stated that the average person uses only ten percent to fifteen percent of his or her brain's potential. It now appears that this figure is too high. It is thought that we do not use even one percent of our mental potential. It seems that the limits of the human brain are only determined by the limits to which we use it, and the limits of what we believe to be possible. For example, its storage capacity is sufficient to record a thousand new bits of information every second from birth to old age and still have room to spare.

Recent experiments suggest that we may remember everything that happens to us. Dr. Wilder Penfield, a neuropsychologist, stimulated the brain with electricity and discovered that touching different parts of the brain resulted in people recalling things that happened at an earlier age, even as young as six months. Amazingly, they were able to describe the scenes in great detail.

In spite of the vast amount of information being discovered now about the brain's fantastic capacities, few people know how to make the most of it. This is partly due to the fact that even though there are books on subjects such as cooking, sewing, pets, travel, car and television repair, health, diet, exercise, and more not nearly enough is written for the general public on how the brain works and how to use it to your advantage.

Scientists still have much to learn about how to maximize the brain's potential in studying, reading, memorizing, and other daily tasks. They have made some interesting discoveries, however, concerning ways to improve the general health and fitness of your brain. Let's look at what these findings mean to you.

Use It or Lose It

One crucial factor in improving the fitness of your brain is that of continued use. For many, graduation from school signals a decline in the use of the brain. Along with this comes a decline in the brain's potential. Like anything else, the brain atrophies if not used consistently. Think of it in terms of your car. If you use the car daily, it starts easily. If you let it sit for a year, the battery runs down, and you need a jump-start to get the car going. Like the car battery, your brain "runs down" if not used regularly.

In order to increase the efficiency of your brain, it is also crucial to continue to experience and enjoy mental challenges. Such a challenge could be as simple as doing the crossword puzzle in the newspaper. Other challenges include taking classes, workshops or seminars. Challenges that are fun, interesting, and free from stress work best.

The third crucial factor is the need to exercise your brain on a regular basis. You can do this by examining more closely the things around you. Allow yourself to become aware of trees, flowers, colors, buildings, furnishings, clothing, expressions on people's faces, etc. Being aware of your surroundings in this way has been shown to increase the thickness of the cerebral cortex which houses the higher thought processes of your brain.

Remember, your brain deteriorates from disuse, not from age!

Regular, physical exercise is also a crucial part of caring for your brain. On a short-term basis, it increases the oxygen supply to your brain which increases mental alertness and creativity. On a long-term basis, it helps keep your arteries clear. In addition, regular exercise increases emotional stability, imagination, and self-sufficiency.

Regular rest periods are necessary to keep your brain functioning efficiently. Research has shown that your production is increased when you take a ten-minute break every hour. You can accomplish more by working for fifty minutes, taking a ten-minute break and working for an additional fifty minutes than you can by working straight through for two hours.

Along with rest, deep relaxation has been shown to lead to fuller use of your mental potential. The deep breathing experienced during relaxation increases the blood supply to your brain which enhances creativity.

A well-balanced diet high in vitamin E is another means of increasing the amount of oxygen in your brain. Mental alertness is also increased by a diet rich in whole wheat grains, sunflower seed oil, vitamins B, C, and D, and fresh vegetables and fruits. It has been found that it is best to avoid artificial preservatives and dyes since these are harmful to your brain. Too much sugar and starch can lead to mental dullness as evidenced by that sleepy feeling you get after a meal that is heavy in carbohydrates and light in protein. Excessive caffeine, alcohol and some drugs also result in mental dullness.

It is important, then, that you use and care for your brain just as you use and care for the rest of your body. The benefits are tremendous. In the next section, we will examine the inner workings of the brain.

THE TWO SIDES OF YOUR BRAIN

Interest in the brain dates back at least to the time of the ancient Greeks. As early as 400 B.C., Hippocrates recognized the brain as the center of man's thinking processes. In the seventeenth century, René Descartes, a French philosopher and mathematician, spoke of the two hemispheres of the brain. He theorized that they act together to help people perceive a unified mental world.

In the 1860s, Broca, a French neurologist, along with Wernicke, a German neurologist, made an important discovery. They found the two sides of the brain have distinctly different functions.

Later in the 1880s, John Huglings Jackson, an English neurologist, described a patient who had right-brain damage and loss of visual perception. He stated that the right side of the brain appeared to be specialized for pictures, while the left side appeared to be specialized for language.

Almost a hundred years later, in the 1960s, Nobel prize winner Roger Sperry of the California Institute of Technology verified these observations in his work on patients with epilepsy. He severed the corpus collossum, the bridge that separates the two sides of the brain. Although the two sides of the brain could not communicate with each other, he found they each continued to perceive, think, and try to control behavior. He also found the right side to be superior to the left in spatial tasks, but inferior in verbal tasks.

Recent research during the 1970s and 1980s has given us even deeper insight into the workings of the two sides of the brain. We now know that each side of the brain processes information quite differently. However, even though the left and right hemispheres work in unique ways, they are both equally important.

Jerry Levy, biopsychologist of the University of Chicago, Illinois, is quoted in the May 1985 issue of *Psychology Today* as saying, "Logic is not confined to the left hemisphere. There is no evidence that either creativity or intuition is the exclusive property of the right hemisphere. Indeed, real creativity and intuition, whatever they may entail, almost certainly depend on an intimate collaboration between the two sides."

To tap most effectively into the almost limitless potential of your brain, you first need a clear understanding of how it works. In the next section, you will explore how each side of the brain thinks and processes information, and how you can use the specialties of each to get what you want faster and easier.

Characteristics of the Left and Right Brain

The first step in learning to use your left and right brain more effectively is to understand the characteristics of both, and see how they differ from each other.

The left brain uses words and numbers very effectively. You are conscious of thoughts from your left brain. It knows what should be done first, second, third, etc. When drawing con- clusions, it works with logic, and puts details together in an organized way to give you a complete understanding of a situation.

The left brain takes a small bit of information, such as knowing one football player well, and generalizes that all football players are like the one who is well known.

Time is of the essence to the left brain. It feels the importance of watching the clock and keeping on schedule. Examples of people who utilize the left brain's functions very effectively are accountants, lawyers, and mathematicians.

The right brain has very little connection to words. It commu- nicates through pictures rather than words. From these images, you get hunches and feelings about things. Very often you are not aware of your thoughts from the right side of your brain.

Instead of being logical or sequential as the left brain is, the right brain starts anywhere when dealing with a project. If you begin washing and waxing the car totally from the right side of your brain, you might start putting the wax on before you have washed the car.

Rather than seeing the parts of a project like the left brain, the right brain sees the whole picture in a situation. It makes great leaps of insight by processing hunches, visual images, feelings, and many other small bits of information as it relates to people and things in the present moment. It is able to deal with many things at the same time.

Logical facts are not needed by the right brain when drawing conclusions. It just "knows" the answer. It is also able to synthesize information from many different sources and come up with something new and different.

Time means nothing to the right brain. It likes to do something until it "feels finished" rather than doing something for an hour and stopping when the clock shows the time to be up. Examples of people who utilize the right brain's functions very effectively are musicians, sculptors, and inventors.

Characteristics of the Left Brain	*Characteristics of the Right Brain*
1. Uses words to name and describe things; uses numbers to count things.	1. Very little connection to words.
2. Takes things that are out of order and puts them into order . . . first, second, third, etc. Monitors tasks to see that they are done in order.	2. Starts anywhere. If all the materials were out to wash and wax the car, the right brain might start waxing the car before washing.
3. When solving a problem, starts with separate details and puts them together to get the whole picture. Figures things out step-by-step.	3. Sees the whole picture. Makes great leaps of insight by processing many small bits of information.
4. Takes a small bit of information and applies it to the whole category, such as knowing one football player well, and then applying the qualities of that player to all football players.	4. Relates to things and people as they are in the present moment. Does not connect people or events now to similar events in the past, but accepts a person at "face value" for who he or she is right now.
5. Draws conclusions based on facts and logic.	5. Sees the general picture and is aware of patterns. Synthesizes things. Doesn't require facts or reasons . . . just "knows."
6. Time is important.	6. No sense of time.

The authors do not mean to give the impression that people are either left-brained or right-brained or that one side of the brain is superior to the other. All people use both sides of the brain, although it appears that some display a preference for the left or right brain in the way they function. Neither side of the brain is superior to the other. In fact, almost all tasks are facilitated by a wise use of the "whole brain" approach.

THE FOUR QUADRANTS OF YOUR BRAIN

(Before reading this section, you may want to turn to page 28–31, Identifying Your Brain Quadrant Preference, to see if you prefer to use one quadrant of your brain over another.)

In addition to the brain being divided into right and left sides, each side is divided into two sections. You have an upper right, lower right, upper left and lower left section or quadrant of your brain. Each quadrant processes information a little differently.

Your upper right brain is intuitive and sees the whole picture. It works new information into what you already know. When functioning in this part of your brain, what you do must have personal meaning for you. You enjoy taking the initiative and discovering things. Exploring is fun, and you make up new ideas.

Your lower right brain is very involved with people and feelings. When functioning in this part of your brain, you love to talk, listen and share ideas about things in which you are emotionally involved. You enjoy moving around and interacting with people and things. You want to experience your subject rather than hear about it.

Your upper left brain looks for the facts and weighs and measures things to determine how logical they are. When functioning in this section of your brain, you absorb knowledge and create theories based on logical data.

Your lower left brain tends to details, and organizes everything so that things are done in the right order and are well planned. When functioning in this part of your brain, you evaluate what you have heard and test the soundness of the ideas through implementing them and practicing what you have learned.

Just as you do not work exclusively from one side of your brain, you do not work exclusively from one quadrant of your brain, either. Rather, you integrate the four quadrants of the brain based on the task. If you find you have a weakness in any of the four quadrants, it is possible to develop the skills necessary to strengthen that quadrant.

Example: Does Your Left Brain Know What Your Right Brain Is Doing?

Mary was originally a business client of Lynéa's who later came for help in dealing with a skin rash that had persisted for a year-and-a-half. She had gone to a prestigious hospital, received special treatments, and had been put on strong medication. However, the rash got worse, and Mary began waking up in the middle of the night scratching her arms. During the day, her skin burned and itched unbearably. Medication was increased with no visible improvement. Injections of cortisone were given from time to time to provide temporary respite from the pain and itching. The rash spread to cover her face and legs. In an effort to improve the condition, foods were eliminated from her diet. Now in addition to itching and scratching, there was the added discomfort of being deprived of certain foods. In spite of the medication, she still scratched her way through the day. As she made sales presentations, prospects interrupted her with questions like, "Do you have poison ivy?" Their attention was diverted from the product because of Mary's frequent scratching.

When Mary came to Lynéa for help, she was at her wit's end. Mary was asked to think about the process that was going on. As she thought about it, it went like this:

- My skin itches.
- I scratch.
- My skin bleeds.
- I put medicine on my skin.
- The medicine burns.
- I wake up at night scratching.
- I'm cranky the next day from lack of sleep.

- I'm embarrassed about my rash.
- Some prospects are more interested in my rash than my product.
- The pills make me dizzy.
- I'm at my wit's end.
- I hurt!

When she got to the statement, "I hurt," a flood of tears burst forth. She sobbed and sobbed. Over and over she cried, "I hurt. I hurt. I hurt."

Years earlier, Mary had gotten a divorce from her husband. When they discussed divorce, he swore he would never love anyone else. Although she was the instigator of the divorce, this pleased her. It did not take very long after the divorce, however, for Mary's former husband to find someone else, remarry, and appear to be very happy.

In addition to feeling hurt over his ease and speed in replacing her in his life, Mary felt guilty about being divorced. Lynéa advised Mary to take some time to recognize the hurt buried deep within her, and to comfort herself. She helped Mary's left brain become aware of what her right brain was telling her through the physical condition. Within a few days of doing this, Mary's skin was healed.

The right brain is a storehouse of decisions, feelings and information of all kinds. It has very little connection to words, and therefore expresses itself in ways that are puzzling until you become more skilled at deciphering the right brain's messages.

Mary was not consciously dealing with her feelings of embarrassment and hurt regarding her divorce. Instead, her right brain was expressing "I hurt" in a physical manner, rather than as a verbal message.

Understanding the Right Brain's Message

The right brain's message may be understood by simply allowing an insight to pop into your mind. Another way of understanding the right brain's message is to decipher it by doing the following four steps:

.. List the action steps you go through in as few words as possible. (As Mary did on pages 24 and 25.)

2. Use the simplest words possible to describe what happened or is happening.

3. Imagine you are making this list of actions simple enough that a five-year-old child could understand what is being said.

4. At the end of the list, be sure to include how you are feeling about what has been happening.

Once the hidden part of the experience that is known by your right brain becomes conscious to your left brain and is fully experienced, there is no longer a need to act it out in non-productive or hurtful ways.

CHECKING FOR UNDERSTANDING

Understand How Your Subconscious Works

1. Your subconscious is your mind.	T	F
2. Your subconscious is directed by your brain and nervous system.	T	F
3. Your subconscious strives to achieve images created in your imagination.	T	F
4. Your subconscious produces goals you have consciously chosen.	T	F
5. You must relax as you program your subconscious.	T	F
6. You subconscious needs precise goals.	T	F
7. Without clear goals, your subconscious gives you an average of your past achievements.	T	F
8. Your subconscious evaluates, judges, and thinks for itself.	T	F

9. Your subconscious doesn't follow orders very well. T F

10. You can dissolve any idea in your subconscious you no longer want to believe. T F

11. If there are conflicting ideas in your subconscious, it acts on the dominant idea. T F

12. You can force your subconscious to produce results. T F

13. Your subconscious works only forty hours per week. T F

14. You can change your results by changing your ideas. T F

15. You only have to think thoughts once to have them accepted by your subconscious. T F

16. You don't have to have any feelings about your goals. T F

17. Your mind can't tell the difference between reality and imagination. T F

18. You have to give your subconscious time to solve your problem. T F

19. Your subconscious doesn't know any more about how to reach your goal than your conscious mind does. T F

20. There is a tattooing effect on your brain for every action you have performed in the past. T F

21. You can't produce the tattooing effect on your brain by just imagining. T F

22. Both sides of your brain work in the same way. T F

23. Your creativity is enhanced when using both sides of your brain. T F

24. Your left brain deals with details and puts them together to form the whole picture.   T   F

25. Your right brain has a good connection to words.   T   F

26. The right brain often acts out what is happening.   T   F

27. You can choose whether or not to use your subconscious.   T   F

28. You retain just as much when you hear something once as you do when you hear something six to eight times in a week.   T   F

29. Your brain deteriorates with age.   T   F

Answers:

1. F	5. T	9. F	13. F	17. T	21. F	25. F	29. F
2. T	6. T	10. T	14. T	18. T	22. F	26. T	
3. T	7. T	11. T	15. F	19. F	23. T	27. F	
4. T	8. F	12. F	16. F	20. T	24. T	28. F	

IDENTIFYING YOUR BRAIN QUADRANT PREFERENCE

Directions: Circle the number of each statement that is true of you.

1. I am intuitive.
2. I like to take the initiative.
3. I enjoy discovering new things.
4. What I do must have personal meaning for me.
5. I enjoy being involved with people.
6. I like being involved in activities about which I have strong feelings.

7. I love to talk and share ideas with others about things in which I'm emotionally involved.

8. I like to physically move around frequently.

9. I want to experience a subject rather than hear about it.

10. I enjoy dealing with the facts and details about things in which I'm involved.

11. I weigh and measure facts to determine how logical they are.

12. I absorb knowledge like a sponge soaks up water.

13. I create theories based on logical data.

14. I enjoy tending to the details in a situation or project.

15. I am good at putting things in their right order.

16. I am a good organizer.

17. I evaluate what I hear.

18. I test the soundness of what I learn by using the information personally.

19. I have a good imagination.

20. I enjoy taking risks.

21. I work best when I have an overview of the whole project.

22. I function best in harmonious surroundings.

23. I adapt easily to changes.

24. I like things to be perfect.

25. I like things to be predictable.

26. I work best in a structured environment.

27. It is easy for me to be disciplined.

28. I like working with tasks that require precision.

29. I am good at arguing my point. (This doesn't mean getting angry.)

30. I enjoy mathematics.

31. I am comfortable working on projects where the guidelines are vague.

32. I am impulsive.

33. I enjoy creating experiments.

34. It is easy for me to feel what someone else is feeling.

35. It is easy for me to trust myself and others.
36. I must have drama in my life.
37. Music is a must in my life.
38. It is easy for me to control my emotions and behavior.
39. I tend to take charge of situations and groups.
40. I have strong opinions about whatever I'm involved in.
41. I am persistent.
42. I like digging into the facts.
43. I like handling the technical side of a project.
44. I like to deal with things and people on a rational basis.
45. I am good at analyzing situations and data.
46. I enjoy dealing with people in a formal manner.
47. I have a high need for visual stimulation.
48. I am good at putting jigsaw puzzles together.

Directions: Now circle the same numbers on the chart below that you circled on pages 28, 29, and 30. Ideally you will circle many of the statements and be using all four quadrants of your brain. If there are many more numbers circled in one section than in others, this indicates a preference for functioning from that quadrant of your brain. If there are sections with few numbers circled, you may want to develop those skills and behaviors.

To do this, repeat the uncircled statement on a daily basis. Once that idea is accepted by your subconscious, you will find yourself learning new information or getting involved in experiences that lead to the strengthening of that particular item. As you will learn in later Secrets, your subconscious doesn't need you to tell it *how* to produce the result. It just needs to know what it is you want.

Upper Right Brain Functioning	Lower Right Brain Functioning	Upper Left Brain Functioning	Lower Left Brain Functioning
1	5	10	14
2	6	11	15
3	7	12	16

4	8	13	17
19	9	28	18
20	22	29	25
21	23	30	26
31	24	42	27
32	34	43	38
33	35	44	39
47	36	45	40
48	37	46	41

RECALLING RESULTS AND EXPERIENCES THAT ILLUSTRATE YOUR SUBCONSCIOUS AT WORK

Directions: On a separate sheet of paper, do the following:

1. List results you have achieved very easily.

Examples:

- You said you wanted a quick, easy sale and someone walked into the showroom that same day and bought.
- You put an ad in the paper and rented the house the first day.
- You bet someone you could bag a deer during hunting season and got one.
- You went out to buy a specific piece of clothing and found it at the very first store.

2. List experiences in your life when you really wanted something to happen, yet felt certain it wouldn't and it didn't.

Examples:

- Your agency offered a bonus trip to an exotic vacation stop. You had sold enough to qualify for the trip in the past, but

31

doubted that you could do it again. As you feared, you didn't get the trip.

- You had a sales interview where the prospect said he would buy in thirty days. He gave you his word he would follow through. You wanted him to, but deep down doubted that he would, and he didn't.

IDENTIFYING RESULTS YOU WANT TO DISSOLVE

Directions: On a separate sheet of paper, list situations in your life that you want to stop experiencing. The following are offered as examples. To dissolve the situations you list, write positive denials and affirmations as presented in Secret Two.

Examples:

1. You almost make a really big sale, but it falls through in the end.
2. Over and over it looks like you're going to earn a great bonus, but you are always just a little short.
3. You hire people who have great promise, but turn out to be mediocre performers.
4. You don't have enough time to enjoy your hobbies.

POSITIVE AFFIRMATIONS

Directions: Repeat these affirmations on a daily basis to internalize the principles of your subconscious and hasten the achievement of your desired results.

1. I'm excited to know that the most powerful, creative instrument in the whole universe is my subconscious. It is a wonderful, goal-striving mechanism used by my

brain and nervous system to achieve the clear-cut goals I have chosen.

2. I'm amazed that my subconscious never sleeps, and I'm happy that it is always busy producing the mental images I have created in my imagination.

3. It's easy for me to relax, because my subconscious always steers me in the right direction to achieve my goals. It helps me be in the right place at the right time, saying and doing the right things.

4. I do my part by setting clear-cut goals with precise amounts and specific criteria.

5. Because my subconscious takes what I say literally, I am careful to talk about things as I want them to be.

6. Since "What I See Is What I Get," I happily take the time to make tangible pictures of what I want.

7. Looking at my pictures help me rev up feelings of excitement, joy, relief, desire, pride, determination, and passion about my chosen goals.

8. If I have a problem, I get all the facts together about the goals I have set, then relax to give my subconscious the incubation time it needs to achieve a goal or solve a problem.

9. I dissolve limiting beliefs and information from my subconscious with ease.

10. I efficiently keep written records of my goals and the dates for their achievement. When I reach my goal sooner than my target date, I upgrade my goal, or decide to take time off to celebrate.

11. Since my subconscious acts on my most dominant thought or belief, I relax, knowing that my dominant thought is always the successful, efficient achievement of my goals.

12. I feel confident about reaching my goals because my subconscious is my obedient servant. I always allow it to produce results quickly and easily.

THE
SECRETS
OF
SUPERSELLING

Secret Two

Program Your Subconscious

PREVIEW OF SECRET TWO

PROGRAM YOUR SUBCONSCIOUS

The first step toward superselling is to identify the specific characteristics of your goal. Just as it is nearly impossible to hit a target that is fuzzy or unclear, it is equally difficult to achieve a vague or general goal.

Jeff had a vague goal of wanting to branch out in his career. He had been sending out resumes for more than a year with no positive results. After setting a specific goal and applying the information from the other Secrets, he achieved his career goal in less than thirty days.

In this Secret you will learn how to program your subconscious for specific results.

PROGRAM YOUR SUBCONSCIOUS

PROGRAMMING FOR SUCCESS

As you learned in Secret One, your subconscious plays an important role in helping you achieve the results you want in life. As your obedient servant, it works day and night to obtain both your consciously- and unconsciously-created goals. To get what you want in your life, it is important that you program your subconscious by following these three steps:

1. Identify specific details of your goal
2. Identify unwanted thoughts and feelings about reaching your goal
3. Program your subconscious to empty any unwanted thoughts and feelings and achieve your goal

IDENTIFY SPECIFIC DETAILS

The first step in programming your subconscious is to make the characteristics of your goals as clear and precise as possible. Just as it is nearly impossible to hit a target at which you have not aimed, it is equally hard to achieve a vague goal. Often when people list the specific details they want in a house, car, personal relationship, etc., they get overwhelmed and think the following:

- "I'll never find a house in that price range with that many bedrooms, etc."
- "They don't make a car in that price range with all those luxuries!"
- "I'll be alone forever if I try to find someone with all those traits!"

The truth is just the opposite. The more specific you are in your criteria, the easier it is for your subconscious to achieve your goal. Let's say you have a desire to go on vacation. You walk around saying, "I want to go on vacation. I sure need a vacation. One of these days I'm going to take a vacation." This is not going to get the job done. It does not have the power of the following thoughts: "I am going to vacation in Cancun. I will fly on _____ airline, and stay at _____ hotel for seven days. It would be nice to be out of the snow in February, so I'll plan my vacation for then. I will need $ _____ for the vacation, so I will set $ _____ aside each month until February."

The following two examples further illustrate the importance of specific programming. The first example shows the frustration of vague programming and the kind of results that are achieved. The second example shows the benefits of using specific programming in achieving your goal.

Example: Vague Programming = Same Old Car

Bob and Mary wanted to buy a new car. They were undecided about what make and model they wanted. They didn't want it to cost "too much." They needed to get it fairly soon, because their present car was in need of repair. They were hoping to get a "decent" trade-in price for their present car or possibly sell it privately for cash.

Results: Bob and Mary spent many evenings looking at new cars without finding one they both liked. They were afraid to run an ad on their present car in case it sold before they had their new one. As the weeks went by, the dreaded repairs on the old car became a reality. They had to spend over a thousand dollars to keep it running. This expense forced them to temporarily abandon their search for the new automobile.

Example: Specific Programming = Brand New Wheels

Sylvia and Bert also decided it was time to buy a new car. However, they realized the importance of programming exactly what they were looking for prior to their search. They sat down together and came up with the following list of specific results they wanted to achieve.

1. Own a new car on or before March 10.
2. Spend no more than $20,000.
3. Monthly payments of $500 or less.
4. No less then $3,000 trade-in for their present car.
5. Car must be a white, four-door, family-sized car with tan interior, whitewall tires, automatic transmission, cruise control, tilt steering wheel, reclining seats, air conditioning, radio, and tape deck with automatic reverse.

Once they had programmed the exact results they wanted, their subconscious minds went right to work. Two weeks later, after going to only two dealerships, they were the owners of a new car that fit their specifications exactly . . . even to the monthly payment and trade-in figures.

Besides applying the Secret of being specific in their programming, Sylvia and Bert applied the Secrets of creating a tangible picture, focusing on the end result, and creating a positive magnetic energy field to assist their subconscious in getting them exactly what they wanted. (These ideas are covered in Secrets Three and Four.)

You may think that achieving the results described in the preceding example is easy compared to making sales. However, it is just as easy for your subconscious to find qualified prospects who buy as it is to find your ideal new car.

IDENTIFY ANY UNWANTED THOUGHTS AND FEELINGS ABOUT REACHING YOUR GOAL

If you have a cup full of coffee, and you'd like a cup of tea instead, you must first pour out the coffee. The same is true of your subconscious. If you want to program it for new goals, you must first empty it of the negative beliefs you currently hold concerning those goals. Therefore, the second step in programming your subconscious to help you reach your goals is identifying any thoughts and feelings that may block your success. Begin by thinking about each specific detail of your goal. Be aware of any negative reactions related to reaching your goal and list them on a sheet of paper. You will use this information in the next step.

PROGRAM YOUR SUBCONSCIOUS TO EMPTY ANY UNWANTED THOUGHTS AND FEELINGS AND ACHIEVE YOUR GOAL

To empty your mind of unwanted thoughts and feelings, write Positive Denial Statements about the programming you want to erase. The dictionary gives these definitions for "denial":

1. The refusal to admit the truth of a statement or charge.
2. The refusal to acknowledge a person or thing.

It is very likely that you have areas in your life where you already use Positive Denial Statements successfully. Many people say, "I always go out with my hair wet in the winter, and I never catch a cold," or "I eat all I want, and I never gain weight." By declaring, "I never catch a cold when my hair is wet," they are refusing to admit the truth of the generally held belief, "You catch cold when your hair is wet." Refusing to admit the truth of other people's realities, or refusing to acknowledge their beliefs through the daily use of Positive Denial Statements, wipes the unwanted programming from your subconscious.

In addition to clearing unwanted thoughts and feelings from your subconscious, you program it with the specific goals identified in Step 1. You do this by writing a Positive Affirmation about each goal.

The dictionary gives these definitions for "affirm":

1. To declare positively or firmly.
2. To maintain to be true.
3. To strengthen.
4. To make firm.

Affirmations state the results you wish to achieve. Since your subconscious takes you literally, word your affirmations as if you have already achieved your result. For example, in identifying the characteristics for your Class A Prospects, you write, "I have completed my list of characteristics for my Class A Prospects," rather than, "I am putting together a list of characteristics for my Class A Prospects." The first affirmation programs you to *get the job done* while the second programs your subconscious to *continue the process* instead of completing it.

Once you have identified the characteristics for your Class A Prospects, and any unwanted thoughts and feelings related to reaching your goal, you program your subconscious using this information. There are a number of ways to do this. For best results, use all of them. You can write your personally designed Positive Denials and Affirmations as a list or in a paragraph and read it out loud daily. You can make a tape of them, and play it on a daily basis. This can be played as you are getting ready for work, driving in your car, at your office or home, or just before you go to sleep. You do not have to pay conscious attention to this tape; however, it is crucial that you play it and stay within listening distance until it is finished. You will also have to update your tape from time to time as you reach your goals and identify new information you wish to program into your subconscious.

The Picture-Frame Process is helpful in creating any goal

you *don't consciously know how to reach.* It works for jobs, sales, prospects, weight reduction, buying cars . . . clothes . . . homes . . . finding a physician, choosing the right college, getting a reliable mechanic, locating the right baby-sitter, choosing the correct stock in which to invest . . . the list is endless. As you use this process to achieve goals quickly and easily, you experience less stress, and find you have gained valuable time.

In using this process, you write the specific characteristics identified in Step 1 around the outside of a rectangle so that it makes a picture frame as shown below. Use a large piece of paper so you can write all the characteristics around the edge.

➡ **Write your specific characteristics around the edges** ➡

As you repeat the characteristics, and generate the feelings associated with reaching your goal, your subconscious helps you find the right people and situations to achieve your result.

Your subconscious doesn't need you
to tell it how to produce the result.
It only needs to know exactly what it is you want.

The Three-Step-Process as It Relates to Sales

Example: Moving Surplus Inventory Easily

You are a salesperson for a car/truck dealership. It's the end of the season, and there are a number of vans left over. You have been told that a high-priority goal is to move this stock. Your goal has been identified. Now what do you do?

Typically, the dealership would run extra ads in the paper and on TV, put sale signs in the showroom and van windows, offer extra incentives, and possibly cut the price. These are good steps to follow, and they do get results. However, you would get even greater results by utilizing the power of specific programming.

Step 1: Identify Specific Elements Needed to Sell the Vans

Besides relying on the usual actions listed above, it is important that you identify specific elements needed to sell the vans. This will include characteristics for Class A Prospects as well as a time-frame for moving the vans.

When you identify Class A Prospects, you move away from the "shotgun approach" of selling which is time consuming and costly. Instead, you give your subconscious the specific instructions it needs to zero in on your target.

Your list of goals for selling the vans might look like this:

1. Find families who need more space than they would have in a car.
2. Find buyers with incomes of more than $30,000 per year.
3. Find buyers who have good credit ratings or are able to pay cash.
4. Find families who are able to make decisions quickly and easily.
5. Find customers who don't suffer from buyer's remorse once a sale is finalized.

6. Find families who refer me to friends and business associates.
7. Sell all vans within the next sixty days.
8. Sell all vans at _____ % profit or more.

(For more information on identifying Class A Prospects, see *Finding Class A Prospects Easily* in the Guidelines at the end of this Secret.)

Step 2: Identify Unwanted Thoughts and Feelings Concerning Van Sales

The second step in selling the vans is to eliminate unwanted thoughts and feelings. Start by reading over your characteristics for selling the vans. As you do this, you may experience thoughts similar to the following.

1. People with big families who need a large vehicle can't afford one.
2. People who think they want a van often change their minds.
3. Everytime I sell a van, the customer can't get financing.
4. It's like pulling teeth to sell a van.

Step 3: Program Your Subconscious to Eliminate Unwanted Thoughts and Feelings And Achieve Your Goal

Now eliminate unwanted thoughts and feelings from your subconscious by writing positive denial statements about each one. Program your subconscious to achieve your goal of selling the vans by following each positive denial statement with an affirmation that states your goal positively. Your statements might look like this:

1. I no longer believe that the people who have big families and need vans can't afford to buy them. I easily sell to big families with plenty of money.

2. I never sell to people who get buyer's remorse. All my deals go through.

3. None of my deals fall through because my prospects have credit problems. They either have good credit or pay cash.

4. I no longer believe I have to "do it all myself." My clients are so delighted with the product and my service, they enthusiastically refer me to their friends and business associates.

You may repeat your positive denials and affirmations for a week, a month, or longer. There is no predetermined number of repetitions needed to erase old thoughts from your belief system. You may be thinking that positive denial statements are examples of negative thinking, and might program your subconscious negatively. **Positive Denials are not negative statements.** Positive denials are strong statements of your refusal to buy into negative thinking. They must always be followed by your positive affirmations.

Denial Statements must be read aloud,
or put on tape, and heard daily until the
old belief is erased from your subconscious.

Now make a tape of your positive denials and affirmations, and play it on a regular basis until your goal is achieved.

In addition to repeating the positive denials and affirmations, write the characteristics of your Class A Prospects (which you identified in Step 1) in a paragraph such as this: "I now sell easily and quickly to people who need more space than they would have in a car. They have incomes of $30,000 or more, make decisions quickly and easily, and don't suffer from buyer's remorse once the sale is finalized. They have good credit or pay cash for the vans. They are so happy with the vans and the service I provide, they help me sell more by enthusiastically referring me to their friends and business associates."

Once you have repeated the ideas enough for your subconscious to accept your goal, the customers who fit your description of Class A Prospects are drawn to your dealership as if by magic.

You may also meet them at the gas station, store, a party, or other places outside the dealership.

Example: Closing More Sales With Fewer Appointments

David is an insurance salesman who wanted to increase his income. He wasn't sure he would be able to do this however, because he was already working long hours. He believed that increasing his sales would mean calling more people, setting more appointments, writing more applications, etc. He didn't relish the idea of devoting more hours to his business, since he and his fiancée already felt they didn't have enough time together.

What David didn't realize is that by programming your subconscious, you can close more sales while setting the same amount or even fewer appointments. This programming involves eliminating limiting beliefs from your subconscious, and replacing them with thoughts that describe your sales as you want them to be.

Once your subconscious accepts your goal, you get additional ideas for steps to take to reach your goal. Let's look at how David used this process to sell more and work less.

In learning *The Secrets of SuperSelling*, David realized that he was limiting his production by focusing only on single cases, and on sales to people of limited income. *Step 1.* He developed specific characteristics for his ideal clients which included people of higher incomes with larger assets. *Step 2.* He cleared out the ideas he had learned from others, such as "it takes five years to get established in this business," and to double your sales, you must double your effort.

Step 3. He then programmed his subconscious by repeating his positive denials and affirmations. As a result of this programming, he began to close larger sales. He also interviewed people who sold the volume he wanted to sell. He followed their advice on how to reach a higher level of production. Instead of focusing on single sales, he sold policies to families. He also called on people of higher incomes who bought larger policies. In addition to making telephone appointments, he allowed himself to connect with prospects on the golf course, at the races, and in other non-business settings.

As a result of this, David found himself with more time to spend with his fiancée while still meeting his goals of increased income.

Example: Let Your Mind Do the Work

This third story illustrates the benefits of programming your subconscious in solving a housing problem. It is included in this book on selling, because there are times when your production is affected adversely by personal issues. These issues either drain you emotionally or affect your production because of the amount of time spent dealing with them. By using *The Secrets of SuperSelling* to solve personal issues quickly and easily, your production stays at its usual high level.

Cheryl had lived most of her life near the ocean, and spent much of her free time at the beach. The longest it ever took her to reach the sea was a thirty-minute trip by car, and for a short period of time, she lived only five minutes from the ocean.

When she began selling, she moved to a large city five hours away from the ocean. Her first apartment was a small one. As her sales increased, she wanted to move to a nicer place. After searching through ads in the paper, and clipping out several that looked appealing, she began her search. She looked at several apartments, but was upset because they were expensive and of poor quality.

At first, Cheryl felt overwhelmed. She thought of the multitude of ads in the paper, and how long it would take to check them out. Since she was single, on commission, and fairly new in sales, she couldn't afford to take time to check out all those ads. Instead of focussing on the step-by-step actions needed to find the apartment, she imagined her perfect apartment and listed the following characteristics:

1. A location that gives easy access to all the major highways.
2. Rent no more than $ _____ .
3. Three bedrooms.
4. White or oatmeal colored carpet.
5. Fireplace.

6. Swimming pool and tennis courts.
7. High enough ceilings for a seven-foot Christmas tree.
8. Self-cleaning oven.
9. Automatic ice maker and frost-free refrigerator.
10. Something that would satisfy that longing for the beach.
11. A look of prosperity.
12. Pleasant, ethical owners and property managers.

It is necessary to be specific in programming your subconscious for desired results. Don't be afraid that including specific details will prevent you from finding what you want. As we said before, just the opposite is true. Vagueness keeps you from reaching your goals. Be specific with your programming. Keep your eyes on the prize, and allow your subconscious to lead you to the desired outcome.

Next, Cheryl emptied her mind of unwanted beliefs and thoughts. She did this by writing down the following beliefs about apartment hunting:

1. "The only way to find the 'right' apartment is to look in the newspaper for ads, cut them out, and go look at lots of apartments to find the right one."
2. "It's going to take me 'forever' to find the right place."
3. "I'll use up so much time getting the apartment, I won't have enough time to reach my sales goals."

Cheryl then wrote the following positive denials and affirmations to clear the unwanted beliefs from her mind:

1. "It's not true that the only way to find the right apartment is to look at lots of them. I can find the right one quickly and easily."
2. "It won't take me forever. I'll find it by the date I set."
3. "I'm not worried about not making my sales goals. I'll get both the apartment and make the sales."

Cheryl used the picture-frame process to program her subconscious. She visualized her new living space, and experienced the joy and excitement of having all these features be real for her. Then she "forgot" about finding a new place. She went about her regular activities, waiting for an idea of what to do next.

A few days later, as she was going on a sales call, she found she had some extra time, and had a feeling she should drive a little farther up the road. Soon she drove past an apartment complex, and felt an urge to check it out.

As she drove down the winding driveway, she noticed wooden pilings and chains that looked like landscaping you'd find in a beach town. At the bottom of the hill was a bubbling fountain that reminded her of frothy waves as they come crashing onto shore.

Excitedly, Cheryl went to the leasing office, and learned she could afford this beautiful complex. She enthusiastically agreed to look at the available apartments. She was thrilled to find twelve-foot high ceilings in the living and dining rooms, a fireplace, marble vanities, 1,530 square feet of living space, three bedrooms, tennis courts, and a swimming pool. Around the swimming pool were wide boards just like the boardwalk in the beach town she missed so much. The location was great. It was only three miles from a major connecting highway! Of course she moved in right away!

This was the only apartment complex she looked at after turning the project over to her subconscious.

By programming her subconscious with specific details, Cheryl quickly found her apartment, and was able to devote the majority of her time and attention to her sales activity. This kept her sales at their usual high level.

CHECKING FOR UNDERSTANDING

Program Your Subconscious

1. Writing denial statements erases beliefs from your subconscious that you don't want to believe any longer.   T   F

2. A denial statement is one that refuses to acknowledge that something is true.   T   F

3. Your subconscious can't work unless   T   F
you tell it how to get the job done.

4. You don't have to be specific when   T   F
programming your subconscious.

5. Goal achievement can be easy if you   T   F
program your subconscious to be that
way.

6. When you don't know how to find what   T   F
you want, you need to be very specific.

7. There is little possibility of finding   T   F
what you want unless you know where
to look for it.

8. Once you program your subconscious   T   F
to help you reach your goal, you no
longer need to use traditional methods
of selling.

9. Your subconscious works only on   T   F
unconsciously-created goals.

10. You need to tell your subconscious how   T   F
to go about getting what you want.

Answers

1. T	6. T
2. T	7. F
3. F	8. F
4. F	9. F
5. T	10. F

CLEARING OUT UNWANTED
INFORMATION ABOUT SUCCESS

Directions: Examine your general beliefs about success to see if
you have some that might limit your sales. Here are a few
common ones:

1. It is lonely at the top.
2. The higher you are, the harder you fall.
3. You get your neck chopped off if you stick it out.
4. Anything this good can't last. It's just a matter of time before it's gone.
5. If you do it too well, you get stuck with it all.

Directions: Use positive denials and affirmations to change your limiting beliefs as illustrated below. Repeat daily until your goal is achieved.

1. It's not true that it's lonely at the top. People at the top have all the respect and friendship they want.
2. I don't believe the higher you are, the harder you fall. Good planning and smart moves prevent falls.
3. I'm not afraid that I'll get my neck chopped off if I stick it out. I plan well and make wise choices.
4. It's a lie that anything this good can't last. It's not a matter of time before it's gone. This is lasting, and getting better all the time.
5. I no longer believe I'll get stuck with it all if I do it too well. I do my work well, say no when I want to, and set appropriate limits.

Directions: On a separate sheet of paper, list your personal, limiting beliefs about family, job, money, health, friends, age, your abilities, your desires, etc. The following statements are offered to help you identify them.

1. You can't do that because _____.
2. You can't have that kind of position in the company until_____.
3. You can't make that big a sale unless_____.
4. You can't recruit top producers because _____.
5. When you get to be _____ years old, you no longer can_____.

Directions: In addition to limiting beliefs, you may have conflicts about your goals. On a separate sheet of paper, list your conflicts about your goals.

Examples For Sales:

- You want to be a high-producing salesperson, but fear that following up on all those customers would take away too much of your free time.

- You want to call on companies instead of individuals, but don't want to take the time to do your homework and research the companies.

Example for Management:

- You want a high-producing sales force and need to replace some people who aren't producing enough. However, you feel bad about letting them go and wonder if you should give them a little more time and training.

Directions: To design your own positive denials, fill in the blanks with the appropriate endings. Here are a few to get you started.

1. It is not true that_____.
2. I no longer believe_____.
3. I am not_____.

Repeat your positive denials and affirmations daily until your goal is achieved.

DISCOVERING YOUR THOUGHTS AND FEELINGS ABOUT SELLING

Directions: To help you discover your thoughts and feelings about selling, sit down for a few minutes with paper and pen, or a cassette recorder. Write or say anything that comes to your mind about selling. Don't judge your thoughts. Let them flow in any order.

Directions: The following questions are offered to help you discover what you believe to be true about your product, service, or career.

1. What is the average income?

2. How long does it take to be really good in your field?
3. How hard is it to sell your particular product or service?
4. What percentage of sales fall through between the time the customer says yes and you actually get the money?
5. How many phone calls do you need to make to get your required number of appointments?
6. What is your closing average?
7. How long do people stay on top in your field before they start slipping or feeling burned out?

Directions: When you have finished, read or listen to your statements to determine if they are positive, negative, or a mixture of the two. If you identify negative beliefs in your subconscious about selling, erase them with positive denials and replace them with positive affirmations.

CLEARING OUT UNWANTED THOUGHTS AND FEELINGS ABOUT SELLING

Information: Paul J. Meyer is the founder of Success Motivation Institute International, the world's largest personal development company. Mr. Meyer said in one of his speeches, "Do you know that it is just as okay to sell as it is to buy?" Think about it carefully. Where would the world be if nobody sold anything?

You might make a list of all the things you have bought. Think how your life would be different if no one had taken the time to sell you those items. Get in touch with how grateful you are to the salesperson that helped you buy the things you now cherish.

Make a list of the benefits people receive from owning your product or service. Everytime you talk with someone about your product or service, remember how good it is going to be for that person.

Directions: The following are sample positive denials to help you empty your mind of some common thoughts about selling that block achievement. If any apply to you, repeat them on a daily basis for at least thirty days.

1. I don't worry about where my next sale is coming from. I easily draw my customers to me.
2. Selling is not hard. Selling is easy and fun.
3. Salespeople are not cheats and liars. Selling is an honorable profession and salespeople perform a vital service.
4. It may be true that others have to go on ten appointments to get a sale, but that's not true for me. I sell one out of _____ easily and quickly.

CLOSING MORE SALES WITH FEWER APPOINTMENTS

Step 1: Identify specific challenges related to your goal of making more sales with fewer appointments.

1. Write down your present closing average. (Number of appointments or presentations to number of sales—for example: ten kept appointments to one sale = one out of ten.)
2. Choose a closing average that is higher than your present one. If your present average is one out of ten, you might choose one out of eight. Choose a number that you believe, and one you feel you can easily reach. When you've achieved one out of eight, set a new closing average, and continue this until you have reached your ideal closing average.
3. Develop characteristics for your Class A prospects.
4. Decide that you will get appointments in more ways than just telephoning from your office. Write, "It's not true that the only way to get appointments is by telephoning from my office. I connect with Class A prospects at the gas station, store, church, service clubs, etc."
5. Determine how much each appointment is worth to you by dividing your commission by the number of appoint-

ments you had to set to earn that commission. Then divide your commission by the new closing average you have chosen. For example, if you presently get $500 commission for each sale, and your closing average is one out of ten, each appointment is worth $50 to you. If you choose a new closing average of one out of eight, each appointment becomes worth $62 + dollars to you. When your closing average becomes one out of three, each appointment is worth $166 + to you.

6. Decide that you will connect with a person who values your product or service and who has influence with many people. As you get referrals from this person, your closing average will improve. Decide how much help you want the Center of Influence to be to you. (See Guideline For Finding Centers Of Influence at the end of this Secret.)

Step 2. Empty Your Mind of Unwanted Information

If you have been told that the average in your business is ten appointments for one sale, you must empty your mind of this belief. Write a positive denial such as, "I no longer believe it takes ten appointments to get one sale. I now have a sale from eight (or less) appointments." (Always follow the positive denial with an affirmation of what you want to be true.)

As you feel more comfortable with closing one sale in every eight appointments, write, "I no longer believe it takes eight appointments to get one sale. I now get a sale from every six (or less) appointments. I don't waste my time seeing people who don't want and can't buy my product or service. All the people I see are Class A Prospects."

If you have learned to value working hard to achieve results, you will need to empty your mind of that belief. Along with choosing a new closing average, you will need to write, "I no longer believe I have to work hard for my money. It's okay to work smarter and to earn $62 + for each appointment now." (As you change your goal for your closing average, update your income for each appointment.)

If some people have not been keeping their appointments with you, write, "People don't stand me up anymore. Everyone who sets an appointment with me wants to see me, and is there on time."

Step 3. Program Your Subconscious With Specific Goals

Write your new positive denials and affirmations daily or put them on a cassette tape and listen to them each day. As you reach your goal, be sure to change the number of appointments needed from eight to six, four or two, etc. It is important that you continue to listen to your personal denials and affirmations even after you achieve your goals. Feeding your mind is like feeding your body. You must keep doing it on a daily basis.

(The information in Secret Three, Focus On Your End Result, will also help you close more sales with fewer appointments.)

GUIDELINES

In the pages that follow, you will find guidelines for determining the qualities, characteristics, traits, and features for your Class A Prospects, Centers of Influence, Class A Salespeople, Job or Career, Marriage or Relationship, Ideal Living Space, and Car.

Personal areas are included because your feelings about the place you live and the way you look also affect your sales. The guidelines are provided to help you cover all your bases, so that you create your personal and sales goals just the way you want them to be.

As you use the guidelines, be sure to specify what you truly want. Don't settle for "second best."

> *"It is a funny thing about life;*
> *if you refuse to accept anything but the best,*
> *you very often get it."*
> **Somerset Maugham**

GUIDELINES FOR FINDING CLASS A PROSPECTS

Directions: It is important to identify Class A Prospects for your line of sales. On a separate sheet of paper, fill in specific information in each category that is pertinent to your line of sales.

1. Income level of your client
2. Age
3. Occupation
4. Marital status
5. List qualities that are important to you, such as the following:
   Friendly
   Businesslike
   Easy to talk to
   Good credit rating or ability to pay cash
   Friend of someone I know
   Quick decision-maker
   Dependable
   Loyal
   Person who has influence with company
   Person who has influence with fellow workers
   First-time buyer
   Repeat buyer

Write down the amount of money you want and the date when you want it. Then write a paragraph: "I am thankful I am depositing in excess of $ _____ in my bank account by (date you choose) from selling my product or service to people who are _____ ." (List all the characteristics you have identified for a Class A Prospect.) Repeat this often enough for your subconscious to accept it as a goal. Your subconscious now knows what to find for you.

GUIDELINES FOR FINDING CENTERS OF INFLUENCE

Information: A Center of Influence is someone who genuinely enjoys helping others reach their goals, feels good about suggesting your product or service to his or her friends, associates, and/or superiors, and has influence with them. A center of influence is someone whose opinion is respected by others to the point where his or her recommendation results in the prospect buying on the strength of the endorsement.

There are a number of benefits from having a center of influence. Your center of influence saves you time and effort by giving you Class A referred leads. Your closing average is increased tremendously. You also get appointments with people who would not give you an audience if you simply made a cold call.

To determine what you need as a center of influence, you must first set your sales goal. If you sell your product to individuals, your ideal center of influence might be someone who has lived in the community for years. He or she is known and trusted by many. Endorsement of your product by this person means many easy sales for you. If you want to sell a company, your center of influence would ideally be a part of the company, be respected by upper management, and refer you to someone with the power to make a buying decision.

Directions: On a separate sheet of paper, fill in specific information in each category that is pertinent to your line of sales.

1. Sales Goal _____ .
2. What kind of help do you want from your center of influence?
   - Testimonial letter.
   - Introduction to person in the company who can make buying decisions for the whole company.

- Referrals to friends and colleagues.
3. How many centers of influence do you want?

Directions: Once you get the information about your centers of influence, identify any negative thoughts about how hard it might be to find such people. Write positive denials to dissolve these thoughts and affirmations to program the positive result. Then write all the items identified in one through three in paragraph form or picture-frame process as if it is true for you now. Read it daily.

GUIDELINES FOR FINDING CLASS A SALESPEOPLE

Directions: On a separate sheet of paper, fill in specific information in each category that is pertinent to your line of sales.

1. What level of income do you want your salespeople to need and want?
2. What age level do you want?
3. Do you prefer single or married salespeople?
4. List the traits that are important to you such as the following:
   High ego need to make the sale
   Able to accept constructive criticism
   Able to follow directions
   Likes to take the initiative
   Dependable
   Punctual
   Self-confident
   Self-reliant
   Persistent
   High achievement drive
   Positive self-image
   Empathy
   Sense of humor
   Creative

Loyal
Team player
Desire for large income
Professional appearance

5. How many salespeople do you want?
6. What awards or company recognition do you want for yourself and your sales force?

Once you have completed these, write the information in a paragraph such as, "I'm excited that I have _____ (insert number here) salespeople who produce _____ (insert sales quota here) each month (week, quarter, etc.) They are _____ , _____ , _____ (insert qualities identified in #2,3,4 here.) As a result of our good production, we are _____ (insert recognition here such as being number one in the region, etc.)."

A completed paragraph might look like this: "I'm excited that I have ten salespeople who each produce twelve or more sales each month. They are self-confident, punctual, dependable, empathetic, creative, and have a high ego need to make the sale. They accept constructive criticism easily, follow directions, and are team players. As a result of our good production, we are number one in the region." (Read this paragraph daily and use it in conjunction with the End-Result picture you will make in Secret Three.)

GUIDELINES FOR CREATING A JOB OR CAREER

Directions: One of the factors that enhances sales is having the ideal work environment. Use the following guidelines to aid you in creating your ideal work environment. Write pertinent details for each item on a separate sheet of paper.

1. Clothing: What kind of clothing do you prefer to wear—casual, dressy, sophisticated, comfortable, distinguished?
2. Schedule: Do you prefer a nine-to-five routine or do you like to set your own hours?

3. Physical Activity: Do you prefer to sit, stand, walk around, ride in a car? You may want to sit all day. You may want to have all four options mentioned.

4. Inside or Outside: Do you prefer to be inside most of the time or outside?

5. People or Things: Do you prefer to work with people only? Things only? A combination of the two?

6. Income Desired: Be sure to write the income you desire. Even if you don't think you can earn that income this very moment, your subconscious can find work for you that has the potential to bring you your desired income.

7. Work Routine: Do you enjoy doing routine procedures or do you like to do something new and unpredictable?

8. Climate: Write down your ideal climate.

9. Geographical Area In Which You Wish To Live: Write down the location where you prefer to live.

10. Noise: What level of noise do you prefer? Do you want to hear people, machines, music? If you choose any kind of noise, be specific. If you choose music, do you want to hear the radio, live performers, instruments only, country music, easy listening music? Be specific.

11. Level of Responsibility You Wish To Handle: Do you want minimal, average, or high, executive-level responsibility? What kinds of activities do you wish to manage? Do you want to be responsible for yourself only or for the results of others too?

12. Style of Architecture Desired in Work Environment: Modern, contemporary, traditional, lots of glass, natural light, fluorescent light, etc.

13. Qualities You Want In Your Boss Or Supervisor: List all the traits you like such as sense of humor, fairness, willing to listen to your ideas, etc.

14. Recognition: What kind of recognition do you want for doing well? Do you want money, your picture on the wall, a promotion, a larger territory or extra responsibility?

Directions: Write all the items in paragraph form or picture-frame process as if it is true for you now. Read it daily.

GUIDELINES FOR CREATING A MARRIAGE OR RELATIONSHIP

Directions: A factor that impacts your sales is the quality of your home life. If you are single, the following is offered to assist you in finding your ideal partner so that you are strongly supported in using your potential to its fullest. Fill in the information about each category.

1. What educational level is important to you?

2. What age range?

3. What race, culture, religion?

4. Height?

5. Weight?

6. Body build . . . muscular, large frame, small frame, etc.

7. Diet: What foods do you enjoy eating? What foods are you willing to prepare? If you love red meat, you may not want a relationship with some one who eats a macrobiotic diet. (Food is often an important part of social affairs. The consumption and preparation of food takes up a considerable amount of time. If your partner is happy eating the same kind of foods you are, this is an experience that you joyfully share, rather than one which may cause disagreements.)

8. Children or no children? If you choose children, are you willing to have your own children? Are you willing to adopt? Are you willing to raise children from a previous marriage?

9. What hobbies do you want to share with your partner?

10. What spiritual values do you want in your partner?

11. How much togetherness do you want? Do you want your partner home every night? Home only on the weekends? Do you want separate bedrooms? Separate beds in the

same room? King-size bed? Separate bathrooms and dressing area?

12. Economic standing: How much money in savings? What level of income do you desire?

13. Tangible assets desired: Think about houses, cars, investment property, other investments.

14. Health: Do you want someone who is healthy so you can enjoy things together? Do you want someone who is sick or has a handicap so you can be of service to that person? Some people have found great fulfillment in being a partner to someone who is an invalid or handicapped.

15. What level of pampering and attentiveness is important to you? If you're a woman, does someone opening your car door warm your heart, or do you feel impatient and resent "having to wait" for the door to be opened? What means pampering to you—flowers, cards, impromptu notes on your pillow? Both men and women like some degree of pampering. How much do you want and what kind? Do you want presents on regular holidays, unexpected surprises on days that aren't holidays or both?

16. Miscellaneous values: How should money be used? How important are savings? How should children be disciplined? Look at your values about work, play, how you get to the top, how you treat relatives, the importance of material possessions to you, etc. What are your values about friends? Is it okay for friends to drop in unannounced, or do you want all visits to be prearranged?

17. Sex: What do you expect and desire sexually?

18. Occupation: Are there occupations that you very much admire? If so, it would be easy for you to support your mate in these careers. On the other hand, if you strongly disapproved of your mate's career, you'd always be a thorn in his or her side. You'd always be wanting him or her to change. This could be the cause of much trouble.

Directions: Write all the items in paragraph form, or use the picture-frame process and read it daily. Once you are clear as to what you want in a mate, your subconscious is able to magnetize to you someone who fits your characteristics.

GUIDELINES FOR FINDING THE IDEAL LIVING SPACE

Directions: A factor that impacts your sales is the quality of your home life. The following is offered to assist you in creating your ideal living space.

1. Do you wish to own or rent?
2. What area of town is desired?
3. How close or far away from major highways?
4. How big a dwelling?
5. Old or new building?
6. Style: contemporary, Spanish, traditional, ranch, town-house, etc.
7. What kind of view? Trees, water, commercial buildings, neon lights, mountains, desert?
8. Families or only adults as neighbors?
9. Age level of your neighbors? Working or retired?
10. How close to schools, shopping centers, hospitals, movies, museums, golf courses, etc.?
11. If renting, list the traits you want in the owners and property managers.
12. Do you have transportation, or does it need to be close to public transportation?
13. Fireplace?
14. Skylights?
15. Tennis court, swimming pool, jacuzzi, etc.?
16. Exercise room?
17. Wall-to-wall carpeting? Hardwood floors? Area rugs?
18. List any other items that are important to you.

Directions: Write all items in paragraph form or use the picture-frame process. "I am thankful that I am living in a place that is _____ , _____ , _____ , etc." Read this daily. See yourself already in this space, and feel how good it would be to live here.

GUIDELINES FOR CHOOSING THE RIGHT CAR

Directions: When choosing a new car, it is important to consider the factors relevant to your line of sales. The following is offered to help you be specific. On a separate sheet of paper, jot down the characteristics that are relevant for you.

1. How much are you willing to spend? How much of a down payment can you afford? How big a monthly payment can you afford? Lease? Own?
2. New or used car?
3. What style: sports car, luxury car, family car? (Do you have to carry inventory in your car? Do you have to carry passengers? Does your line of sales require an "image" car?)
4. What kind of seats: leather, cloth, vinyl?
5. Whitewall tires?
6. Special hubcaps?
7. Is gas mileage a factor for you?
8. What kind of music system?
9. Tape deck? Auto reverse?
10. Air conditioning?
11. How much can you afford to pay for tags and insurance?
12. What size trunk do you need?
13. Do you want to do your own maintenance? If so, how easy is it to get parts? (There may be some items that are important to you that are not included in this list. Do not limit yourself to the items mentioned here.)

Implementation: Once you have decided on all the details, write out a paragraph as if you are already in possession of your car. Read this daily until you get your new car.

Example: "I am thankful I now own my (color) _____ (insert make and model of your choice here). The payments are no more than $ _____ a month. I love my music system, air conditioning, and comfortable, reclining seats. The car is trouble free and needs only regular maintenance. The whitewalls and wire wheels are classy looking. The insurance and tags combined are no more than $ _____. I am glad my previous car covered the down payment. I'm enjoying the deep sound of the Bose music system as I drive from sale to sale."

POSITIVE AFFIRMATIONS

Directions: Repeat these affirmations on a daily basis to internalize the principles of your subconscious and hasten the achievement of your desired results.

1. I program my subconscious to reach my chosen goals easily and quickly by identifying the specific characteristics of my personal and professional goals.
2. I regularly empty my mind of unwanted, limiting information.
3. I use the picture-frame process to help me create any goal I want but don't know how to reach. Then I relax and let my right brain find the missing details.
4. I don't worry about where my next sale is coming from because my positive magnetic energy field easily draws my customers to me.
5. Selling is not hard, and salespeople are not cheats and liars. Selling is easy and fun.
6. Selling is an honorable profession, and salespeople perform a vital service.
7. It may be true that others have to go on _____ appointments to get a sale, but that's not true for me. I sell _____ out of _____ all the time.
8. I have several centers of influence who help me reach my sales goals.
9. It's not true that it's lonely at the top. People at the top have all the respect and friendship they want.

10. I don't believe the higher you are, the harder you fall. Good planning and smart moves prevent falls.
11. I don't believe that good things can't last. My success is lasting, and getting better all the time.

THE
SECRETS
OF
SUPERSELLING

Secret Three

Focus on the End Results

Preview of Secret Three
End Results
Principles of End Results
Checking for Understanding
Identifying Your End Results
Creating Your Tangible Pictures
Positive Affirmations

PREVIEW OF SECRET THREE

FOCUS ON THE END RESULTS

Once you have established your clear, precise goal, Secret Three helps you create end-result pictures related to both personal and professional goals. Research strongly supports the importance of the visual factor in goal achievement and validates the statement, "What You See Is What You Get."

The power of end-result pictures is shown in the story of Susan who wanted to develop a more affluent clientele. As a result of participating in *The Secrets Of SuperSelling Workshop*, she put together a picture book showing the type of clients she wanted. After just ten days of looking at the pictures, she made an appointment at a local beauty salon specializing in make-overs. When they had finished, she was delighted to see that she looked like the pictures of the women in her book. As a result of her new image, she found herself easily doubling her sales as she dealt with more affluent customers.

In Secret Three, you learn how to focus on the end result in addition to carrying out your logical, step-by-step plans for reaching your goal.

FOCUS ON THE END RESULTS

END RESULTS

Now that you have identified the specific characteristics for your goal with the left side of your brain, it is time to bring your right brain into play. You do this by focusing on the end result of your goal. The following are examples of people who have used the end-result process to help them reach their goals.

Example: Within a very short period of time after beginning her career in sales, a woman became one of the best in the nation in her field. At her first training session after joining the company, she noticed that the highest achievers had red ribbons attached to their name tags. She really wanted one of those ribbons, because it would let everyone know that she had done well, and this recognition was important to her.

Yes, she wanted the money from the sales that qualified her for the red ribbon; she also wanted to provide the service to her clients. However, the thing that evoked the strongest emotion within her was the idea of wearing that ribbon at the training meetings and being recognized for high achievement. (Harvard has reported that the number-one motivator of people is the desire for recognition.) She knew the only way to get the ribbon was to produce the required number of sales. By picturing herself in possession of the ribbon she gave her subconscious the task of accomplishing that result. She did not focus on the number of sales needed to qualify for the ribbon. She didn't worry about whether or not she would reach her goal. She focused on wearing that ribbon, and felt the pride and excitement of being one of the top producers. With her desired end result pictured clearly in her mind, she got the number of sales she needed one day before the deadline!

Example: One of the participants in the *Secrets of SuperSelling Workshop* sold $100,000 homes. He wanted to increase his income and work fewer hours. Using the end-result process, he made a tangible picture that showed his desired income along with a calendar on which he blocked out the decreased number of hours he wanted to work each week. Five months later, he exceeded his goal by selling a million-dollar building. He made the same commission with one sale that he usually made with ten sales! He had never thought of selling a million-dollar building; he had no plan to prospect for a sale of that magnitude. However, by focusing on the desired end result of having more income and working less hours, his subconscious linked him up with a million-dollar sale.

Example: Bruce Jenner applied this principle after competing in the Olympic decathlon without even placing. He took a life-size picture of the winner of the event, and put a picture of his face in place of the face of the winner. In addition to following his usual training program, he viewed the picture of himself as the winner each day. *He won the next Olympics in 1976.*

From these examples, you can see the power of focusing on the end result in achieving your goals. Understanding the principles of the end-result process will help you to use it effectively.

PRINCIPLES OF END RESULTS

Principle Number One: Your End Result Must Be One That You Really Want and Have Strong Feelings About

The stronger you desire an end result, the easier it is for your subconscious to create the result for you. If you want to earn $ _____ in commissions or bonuses, (you fill in the amount), you must first identify an end result related to that amount of money that would please you. It must be something you really want, and can put some energy behind. Your end result could be something intangible such as recognition as top salesperson where you work. It could be tangible such as new clothing or a nicer place in which to live. It could be an altruistic goal such as being able to make a donation of a sum of money to a favorite charity. It could be an adult toy such as a new car, boat, VCR, or stereo. The important thing is that it must be something that can only be purchased, obtained or experienced if you earn that amount of money, by producing that level of sales.

Principle Number Two: Your Focus Must Be on the End Result Rather Than on the Steps Needed to Achieve It

By identifying and focusing on the end result, rather than on the steps you take to get there, you open the door to creative new ways to achieve your goal. Take a left-brain approach to earning the income you've chosen. First, compute the average commission you make per sale. Next, figure out how many sales you'd have to make to earn the desired amount. Then, come up with a well thought-out plan to get the needed number of prospects and sales. That kind of planning is necessary, and you will want to continue using it.

In addition, by focusing on your end result of special recognition, the car, house, boat or whatever you've chosen, you include the right-brain way of thinking and problem solving. This opens the door to the possibility of earning the money desired with fewer but larger sales, or in ways that are much easier than you originally anticipated.

Principle Number Three: For Best Results You Must Have a Tangible Picture of Your End Result

From the examples at the beginning of this Secret, you see that visualizing something with strong emotion is a powerful tool in achieving results. Hegel, in *Introduction To Logic*, reports that you always look toward an object before thinking it. It is by looking at the object many times in your imagination that you really begin to know and understand it.

Research supports Hegel's theory by revealing that 87 percent of the impact made on an individual is made through visual means, 7 percent through hearing, 3 percent through touch, 2 percent through taste, and 1 percent through smell. The importance of the visual impact is supported by IBM's survey which found that 56 percent of their sales force accounted for only 11 percent of their sales. This meant that less than half of their sales force accounted for 89 percent of their sales. (They also found that of the 44 percent who accounted for 89 percent of the sales, 2 percent produced 34 percent of the total.) The main difference between the high and low producers in the sales force was that the high producers demonstrated their product. In addition, once they showed their customers their product, they encouraged them to experience the product by handling it. (Research also shows that people are 22 percent more likely to buy a product once they hold it in their hands.)

When they checked the 56 percent of the sales force who made only 11 percent of the sales, they found these people only talked when selling their product.

This and other research solidly supports the power of visual impact in selling, as well as supporting the idea that a major key to programming your subconscious successfully is seeing your goal.

The Importance of Tangible Pictures

Even if you are very skilled at seeing pictures in your imagination, it is suggested that you have some physical symbol of your end result. For your subconscious to draw to you what you desire, it is crucial that you have a steady, clear image that you see over and over again in the same way. If outside factors such as interest rates, the economy, other people's attitudes, etc., predict a negative outcome for you, it is crucial that you have your tangible picture to keep your attention focused on what you want.

To aid in the visualization of your end result, and to capitalize on the strengths of your right brain, put together a tangible picture that represents your end result as precisely as possible.

If you want to sell five homeowner policies in one week, be sure to cut out pictures of five homes. If you want to buy a red car, be sure to have a picture of a red car . . . not a blue one.

> *Tangible pictures are the blueprint that keep your*
> *subconscious focused on your desired result*
> *no matter what may be happening*
> *around you.*

The pictures you create to symbolize your desired result may be photographs, travel brochures, postcards, gummed stickers, or even hand-drawn sketches. It is important that your pictures be bright and colorful.

Putting Yourself in the Picture

Once you've chosen your pictures and cut or drawn them to the appropriate size, arrange them on pieces of paper in a three-ring binder, on a piece of posterboard, or paper of your choosing. As you are arranging your pictures, be sure to put your own photograph in the picture. This helps you feel that it is real, and gets the message to your subconscious that you want this result for yourself! The following ideas will help you create your own pictures.

If you are wanting new clothing, but don't have the money to purchase it, have your picture taken in the clothing you want. Tell the clothing store what you are doing. They are usually happy to help you, for it leads to future sales.

If you wish to double your sales this year, create a picture of you at your company banquet receiving an award for having doubled your sales. You can do this by getting pictures of past award dinners, and putting your picture in place of those being honored. You might also get a photo of your boss handing you your increased commission check.

Scripting the Picture

Somewhere on the page with your pictures, write affirmations appropriate for the end results they represent. Here are some samples:

1. I am now a member of the Million Dollar Club.
2. I am proud to be number one in sales in my company.
3. I'm thankful I am able to give this contribution to_____ .
   (name of charity)
4. I'm thankful I now earn enough money to be able to own
   this _____ .(fill in the item)
5. Our customers are very happy with our product and
   service.

When your pictures are finished, you may want to put them in plastic protectors so they are kept clean and wrinkle-free.

Displaying Your Pictures

It is important to look at your pictures each day. If you live alone, or have people in your home who understand and believe in the importance of what you are doing, you may want to display the pictures in some prominent place. Many people put them on the refrigerator, the bathroom mirror, closet doors, etc., so that they see them on a regular basis.

If you have people around you who are not positive about what you are doing, you may want to keep your pictures hidden from their view. You can do this by putting them in a folder or a three-ring notebook. Look at them every day, until you reach your desired result. It is most effective to do this just before you go to sleep or as soon as you wake up, for your subconscious is most available at these times. Even after you have reached your goal, we recommend that you keep the pictures to remind you of your successes.

Let's Look at Some Examples of End Results in Other Areas of Your Life

It has been the authors' experience that your sales are impacted just as much by how you feel about your life as they are by the amount and quality of sales training you receive.

When you feel good about your weight, you have more energy to apply to your sales goals. Therefore, if you are on a weight-reduction or weight-increase program, see yourself standing on a scale that is showing your desired weight.

When you are physically healthy, you have more energy and enthusiasm for your job. If there is a health problem, see your doctor telling you that you are completely healed. You're fit as a fiddle!

If you have a recurring problem of not having enough money, visualize yourself depositing large checks in your bank account and feeling good about always having plenty of funds. See yourself doing fun things with your money such as owning a boat, going on vacation, going out to dinner, buying a much-desired book, going hang-gliding, etc. If your main focus is on earning just enough to pay bills and waiting until later (when you're *really* successful) to enjoy your money, you are setting up a condition where the Child within you is feeling deprived. This limits your sales while enjoying your money expands your sales.

Use the End-Result Process to Solve Problems as Well as Achieve Goals

Sometimes you are following your well-mapped-out action plan for achieving your goal, and you run into a problem. You can use the end-result process to clear up the problem efficiently. Let's say you have a customer who wants to buy a boat. He has chosen just what he wants, and you start arranging the financing. If a problem arises, such as the bank turning him down, don't try to change this situation by visualizing that bank giving him the loan. (Morally you don't have a right to visualize results involving other specific people unless they have asked you to do so.) Instead, you visualize the end result of successfully closing the sale. See your customer leaving with the boat. The loan may then go through from the bank with which you are having trouble, you may get financing through another institution, or your customer may find financing from some source you have never even considered.

**The main point here is that you don't
want to limit your creativity by visualizing only one
option for reaching your goal.**

> *Your goal is not to get financing from only one*
> *particular bank. It is to close the deal successfully*
> *in a win/win way for everyone.*

Sometimes your left brain wants to run the show by deciding exactly how the goal will be achieved, then trying to force it to happen in just that way. By problem solving from your right brain, you might discover a much better way to get what you want.

> *Take some time with this important process.*
> *Enjoy choosing your end result and*
> *making your tangible pictures.*
> *You are not just making a "picture book."*
> *You are the architect designing your future, and*
> *the end result is part of the blueprint.*

CHECKING FOR UNDERSTANDING

Focus on the End Result

1. When you are using your subconscious, you don't need conscious plans.   T   F

2. You can visualize your end result differently each time.   T   F

3. You must get a picture of the end result you desire.   T   F

4. Once you get an idea of how to go about getting what you want, you insist on getting the result just that way.   T   F

5. It is necessary to follow your hunches and vague feelings once you have programmed your subconscious.   T   F

6. Other people's negative opinions don't have any effect on your results.   T   F

7. It is important that you look at your tangible pictures every day.   T   F

8. Keep your pictures hidden from other people's sight if the people around you are not positive about this activity.   T   F

9. Putting your own picture in the tangible pictures you create makes them more powerful.   T   F

10. You need to make your tangible pictures look exactly like what you want.   T   T

11. You don't need to write any affirmations on your picture.   T   F

Answers:

1. F
2. F
3. T
4. F
5. T
6. F
7. T
8. T
9. T
10. T
11. F

IDENTIFYING YOUR END RESULTS

Directions: On a separate sheet of paper, do the activity suggested in each of the examples that apply to you. These are offered only as samples. Allow your imagination to design others that match goals you want to achieve. Activities are suggested for all areas of your life because your sales results are impacted by the status of your personal and social life as well as your professional life.

Examples:

1. If you want to double your income, list the ways you will use that new amount of money.
2. Describe your dream home.
3. Write down your ideal weight.
4. Describe your net worth and your investment portfolio ten years from now.
5. Describe a scene at the end of the next school year. You and your child are talking over the past school year. Describe it the way you want it to be.
6. Write a press release for a trade journal about your phenomenal increase in profit, productivity, the great results of your Employee Assistance Program, etc. Date the press release for one year from now. Tell it the way you want it to be. Don't worry how you will pull it off.
7. If you are in multi-level marketing, get a copy of your up-line supervisor's bonus check with your name replacing your supervisor's name.
8. Identify something you want to own that you can only get if you increase your income.
9. Fill in the sales board in your company with the sales you'd like to make and take a picture of it.
10. Make up a profit/loss statement for the end of next month that reads the way you want it to read.
11. Decide what kind of recognition you want from your company, then make a mock-up of that. It might be a letter from the president of the company congratulating you on your achievement. It might be your picture in the company newspaper. It might be a promotion or a raise. Don't be limited by these suggestions. Create your own ideas of recognition.

CREATING YOUR TANGIBLE PICTURES

Directions: On a separate sheet of paper, do the activity suggested in each example if it applies to your goals.

1. Describe the financial condition you'd like to be true in your life. Include spending, saving, earning, and investing. Make pictures of your desired financial condition by filling in bank deposit slips with the amount of money you want to be depositing. Fill out a tax return the way you'd like it to be. Take statements from your savings account and change the numbers so that you see the amount of money in your account that you want to have . . . not what is currently there. Get pictures to illustrate the net worth you intend to create and your desired investment portfolio.

2. Get pictures of material possessions you want to own even if you don't have the money to purchase them right now. An example would be to get your picture taken with a boat you want to own, but couldn't buy if your income wasn't at the level you've chosen.

3. To show a budget, do the following: Get fake money at a card store. On a piece of paper, draw separate boxes for utilities, groceries, clothing, car, insurance, church or charity, saving, investing, and any other categories you have in your situation. Put the amount of fake money you wish to spend for groceries in one box, the amount you wish to spend on housing in another box until you have used all your income. (Continue with all the boxes.) Write on this page, "I (We) invest our money monthly in this way."

4. Write a company press release for a trade journal or a report to stockholders about your phenomenal increase in profit and/or productivity, the great results of your Employee Assistance Program, etc. Date the press release for six months or one year from now. Tell it the way you want it to be.

5. Describe a fun activity you'd like to do. If you don't know what you want to do that would be fun to you, get pictures of people who are having fun. Under the pictures write, "I now know what I want to do that would be fun for me, and I let myself do it." If you have photographs of you doing fun things, put these into your picture book and look at them daily.

6. Describe in detail what you would like to do for your family, city, state, country, or the world. Possibilities are to help your family live a richer life, clean up pollution in your city, be mayor, be on the city council, help out in a presidential election, etc. Then get pictures of this result. You might put a picture of your family by a picture of a new home, or your picture over a picture of someone receiving a plaque from your mayor, your picture on a picture of a ground-breaking ceremony for a building someone helped build, or pictures of well-fed children and a caption "No More Starving Children."

7. Describe in detail what you want to do for your church, spiritual group, club or organization. If you want to increase membership, you could cut out pictures from magazines showing the number of people you would like to have in your group, paste them on a piece of paper, and write, "I'm glad we have this many members in our group."

8. Set the counter back on your scale so that it shows your ideal weight. Have your picture taken with the scale showing that weight. Find one of your photographs when you were thinner; or take a picture from a magazine of someone else's body, and cover the head in the picture with your head from a photograph of yourself. Find before and after pictures of someone who did what you want to do (reduce weight, build up muscles, gain weight, etc.) Under that picture write, "I am successful in reducing my weight (building my physique, etc.) just as _____ (the name of the person in the picture) was."

9. Write a story about a large contribution you made to your favorite charity. If possible, have your picture taken with the head person from that charity shaking your hand. If this isn't possible, find a picture of some-

     one being congratulated by that person, and put your picture in place of that person.

10. If you are in real estate and want to be in the Million Dollar Club, get a picture of people being honored at the awards banquet. Put your photograph somewhere in the picture so you are included in the ceremony.

11. Get a travel brochure of a place you'd like to visit. Have your picture taken in clothing appropriate for that trip. Then put your photo in the middle of the picture that really appeals to you.

12. If you want to increase production by 20 percent and lower costs by 15 percent, write a letter to yourself from the president of your company, congratulating you on these specific achievements. Date it a few days later than the target date for your goal achievement. Read the letter daily. Get your picture taken with the president presenting this letter to you.

POSITIVE AFFIRMATIONS

Directions: Repeat these affirmations on a daily basis to internalize the principles of your subconscious, and hasten the achievement of your desired results.

1. I identify end results that stir up strong emotions within me for the goals I want to achieve.

2. I make tangible end-result pictures for the goals I intend to accomplish.

3. I am careful to make my end-result pictures look exactly like what I want, because what I see is what I get.

4. I include my own picture in all my end-result pictures, write affirmations on them, and look at them daily.

5. I allow my subconscious to help me achieve my goals easily.

6. I take action on my conscious plans and follow my hunches for achieving my goals.

THE
SECRETS
OF
SUPERSELLING

Secret Four

Create Your Magnetic Energy Field

Preview of Secret Four
Magnetic Energy Field: Fact or Fancy?
Quantum Physics
Energy Fields Scientifically Proven
Creating Your Magnetic Energy Field
The Power of Your Magnetic Energy Field
Negative Magnetic Energy Fields
How Negative Judgments Happen
The Effects of Negative Judgments
How Positive Judgments Happen
Checking for Understanding
Avoiding Negative Energy
Increasing Positive Energy
Repelling Unwanted Experiences
The Power of No
Identifying and Dissolving Negative Denials
Identifying Negative Judgments
Identifying and Dissolving Fear
Positive Affirmations

PREVIEW OF SECRET FOUR

CREATE YOUR MAGNETIC ENERGY FIELD

Secret Four teaches you to create a Positive Magnetic Energy Field that energizes your goals, attracts to you to the things you desire, and repels from you the things you don't want.

The following example illustrates how easy it is to achieve goals once you have created your positive magnetic energy field.

Stan was new in real estate, and wanted to do well in his business. However, he was an older gentleman who also wanted to spend a great deal of his time helping people, working in his garden, and pursuing other interests that brought him pleasure, but no money. While participating in *The Secrets of SuperSelling Workshop,* he created an internal image of himself earning money while doing the things he loved to do. A short time later, he sold a couple their new home after helping them find their way to the airport. His next sale came when he gave a couple he met a tour of Atlanta before they flew back home. They decided they could save time and money by living in Atlanta, and bought a $300,000 home on the spot.

By creating your own positive magnetic energy field, your goal achievement can be just as easy as Stan's.

CREATE YOUR MAGNETIC ENERGY FIELD

MAGNETIC ENERGY FIELD: FACT OR FANCY?

The idea that each of us has at our disposal some powerful form of energy has been spoken of down through the ages. Most of the major religions of the world mention this power or force as a special gift to be used to our benefit. Buddha taught that people could become so peaceful through using this current that nothing could ever hurt them again. Confucius taught that people would no longer say or do mean things to their neighbors if they used this force. Christian religions speak of a power within each person. In 1 John 4:4 you find, "The power in you is greater than any power that is in the world."

To demonstrate the strength of this inner power, members of the Human Potential Movement have taught their participants to use their thoughts and energy to accomplish such feats as walking barefoot over burning coals unharmed.

Recent scientific discoveries have shed new light on this mysterious power. Many of the ideas about human energy fields that were previously mere speculation are now being found to be real and observable.

QUANTUM PHYSICS

One of the areas of science that has increased our understanding of the special power within us is quantum physics. While the subconscious has long been a mystery to mankind, quantum physics is helping make this creative instrument less mysterious by giving us scientific data that explain its intricate workings.

It is proposed that the pictures you create in your imagination are electromagnetically charged with your energy. They set up a magnetic energy field that pulls to you what you picture, and pushes away from you anything different from what you see in your imagination.

For an explanation of how this works, we look to Dr. Karl Pribram, world-famous neurosurgeon and psychologist at Stanford University. He has been called the Einstein of brain research. He believes that the Hologram Theory, for which Dennis Gabor received the Nobel Prize in 1971, offers an explanation of how the brain sets up this energized picture.

When you look at a tangible picture, your eye acts as a camera, and changes what you see into wave storage, and then into images in your mind. These images are again changed into wave storage and radiated out, drawing the pictured result to you, while pushing away things that are different from these pictures.

What you see is truly what you get.

Because vividness and sensory detail increase the energy and power of the images in your imagination, you want to be very clear and detailed with your goal setting. For instance, you may set a goal to double your production in life insurance sales. To reach this goal, see a crystal clear image in your imagination of yourself closing customer after customer. Picture your sales manager congratulating you as he gives you a commission check that is twice as large as your present check.

The combination of your pictures plus your feelings about them creates your magnetic energy field. This carries your images away from you into the air where they can be picked up by other people. This is similar to television stations transmitting their programs through the air waves, making them available to be received by anyone who has a television set and antenna. The many transmitted pictures are always available, but are only seen when a person turns on the television set, and chooses which channel to watch.

You function like the television station in that you produce and transmit your own pictures. You also function like the television set in that you are able to tune into the pictures being transmitted by others.

ENERGY FIELDS SCIENTIFICALLY PROVEN

Energy fields are scientifically-proven phenomena. Using a process called Kirlian photography, pictures have been produced of the energy field surrounding people and plants. In one experiment, people whose Kirlian photographs showed a break in their energy fields were monitored over a period of time. At some point in the future, they developed an illness in their physical bodies at the same place where the break occurred.

Scientists describe your energy field as light energy that flows in a circuit, travels through space, and performs work. Through repetition of your pictures, thoughts and feelings, a goal is accepted by your subconscious, and your magnetic energy field is created.

This field acts just as magnets do. When you put the ends of magnets near each other, they either push away, or quickly come together. Likewise, your magnetic energy field either pushes away from you or pulls to you those things you have pictured in your imagination and described verbally. (The following diagram illustrates this process.)

Your Magnetic Energy Field

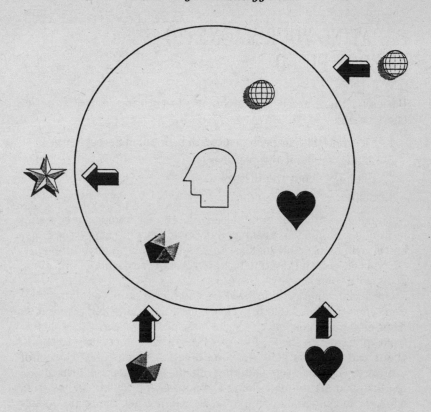

The large circle in the diagram represents your magnetic energy field. The different shapes both inside and outside the circle are symbols representing your goals such as customers, sales awards, income, cars, etc.

CREATING YOUR MAGNETIC ENERGY FIELD

Basically, there are four components in creating your magnetic energy field:

1. Pictures (this has been dealt with in detail in Secret Three).
2. Thoughts about the pictures.
3. Feelings about the pictures.
4. Sound.

The pictures in your mind determine the form your energy will be molded into just as a cake pan determines what shape the cake batter will take. And just as bakers can make many different-shaped cakes with the same batter, you can create many different goals with your energy.

Once your energy is formed by the pictures in your imagination, your thoughts hold it in that particular shape and prevent it from changing, just as the cake pan prevents the cake batter from changing its shape. For this reason, it is necessary to think about and visualize your goals on a regular basis until they are achieved. If you stop thinking about them for several days because you are so busy doing the activity of your business, the energy can change its form, and you will not get the goal you set out to achieve. Keeping your energy in the form of your desired goal is easy. It takes only a few minutes a day to look over your pictures, and to listen to your own positive denials and affirmations about your goals.

The third component in creating your magnetic energy field is feelings. As was mentioned earlier in this Secret, your eye acts as a camera, and changes what you see into wave storage, and then into images in your mind. As you look at these images over and over in your imagination and get strong feelings about them, your feelings change them back into wave storage and radiate them out. If they are not changed into wave storage by your feelings, it is the same as having a powerful piece of advertising composed in your mind, but never changed into a form such as a brochure that can be mailed out to the public.

The intensity of your feelings also determines the strength of your positive magnetic energy field. Weak feelings produce a weak field while strong feelings produce a strong field that can be felt for great distances.

The fourth component in creating your magnetic energy field is sound. For centuries, people have recognized the power of the spoken word. The Babylonians believed that words were either commands or promises which *had* to come true. Eastern philosophies teach that words which are spoken have tremendous power with the spoken or sung word being 80 percent more powerful than the silent word. Sound waves radiate out very much like the ripples in a pond after a stone has been thrown into the water. The sound of your voice propels your images away from you on sound waves so that other people can tune into your pictures. This connects you with people and conditions needed to fulfill your goal easily and quickly.

To create a powerful magnetic energy field, you must use a combination of all four components. It is necessary to look at the tangible picture of your goal on a daily basis. You must write out your thoughts about your goal as if it has already happened, and repeat them out loud each day. You must generate feelings about your desired result while focusing your attention on your pictures.

It is not possible to cut corners here and still get the results you desire.

You must do all the components on a daily basis. Therefore, take a few minutes each day to look at your pictures, say your denials and affirmations out loud or listen to your own personal cassette tape, and get excited about your goals *already* being achieved.

HOW TO CREATE YOUR MAGNETIC ENERGY FIELD

Each time you set a new goal, you'll want to create your magnetic energy field for that goal by doing the following:

Step 1.

Set some time aside in your daily routine to focus your attention on the result you are creating. Pick a spot where you will be uninterrupted. Unplug your telephone. Put a note on your door that you're not to be disturbed. Stillness of body and mind are important. You may want to be outside near water, in a forest, on a mountain, or some other spot in nature. You may be just as happy in a favorite spot in your home or at work. You may choose to be alone, or to have someone with you to help energize your picture.

Step 2.

Get the tangible picture of the end result which you made in Secret Three. As you focus your attention on this picture, dismiss thoughts of other activities that require your time and attention. Once you are focused on this one scene, move on to the next step.

Step 3.

Look at the tangible picture you have made of your end result, and pretend you have a miner's cap on your head. Imagine a powerful bulb in the light on the cap. Focus all available light on the picture.

Step 4.

As you continue to look at your picture, look to your right and down. Get into the feelings of pride, satisfaction, relief, joy, exuberance, etc. that you will feel once you've achieved this result. Hold the feelings for at least thirty seconds. This triggers an image in your imagination just like the one in your tangible picture. As you experience your feelings with more and more desire, the image in your imagination is once again changed into a wave form. This is now catapulted outside your imagination by your feeling energy.

Step 5.

Say your affirmations about your goal out loud with enthusiasm. Remember that you are vibrating the picture away from you so that it can be picked up by people who can help you reach your goals.

Step 6.

Now imagine that the energy you sent out in the form of your picture is returning to you as the real object or experience (clients, sales, car, job, etc.)

Step 7.

Once you feel complete in your energizing of the picture, sit quietly for a while. Listen to your right brain, and follow your hunches. For example, if you get a feeling you should go to a certain place, go with a sense of adventure to see what is there. You may find something or someone who will help you reach your goal. Your subconscious has many avenues available to get the message across to you. Insights may come from books, TV shows, friends, relatives, strangers, newspapers, advertisements, etc. Do not fall into the trap of expecting your insights to come to you in the same way or place each time.

Step 8.

Keep energizing your picture until your goal is achieved. A few times may be enough. On the other hand, you may have to do it many times. Set up a regular schedule for feeding your mind positive information, and energizing your pictures. You might choose to spend the first fifteen minutes after you wake up or just before you go to sleep to do this. Tell your subconscious to block out all noises. Set an alarm clock to let you know when fifteen minutes are up, so that all your attention is focused on energizing your goals rather than worrying about the time.

The first time you energize a major goal (salesperson of the month, car, house, marriage, etc.) it is recommended that you give yourself a day to go to a special place. Take as much time to work on it as you feel necessary. Really get into the experience; make it as powerful as possible. Subsequent energizing of your goals can be handled in the daily programming of your subconscious.

Step 9.

Just as you would not put a favorite photograph outside to be ruined by the weather, do not share the tangible symbol of your end result with people who would react negatively. If you think your friends and family might doubt that you could reach your goals, don't show your pictures or tell them anything about your plans until *after* you have been successful.

It is necessary to continue visualizing, energizing, and affirming your goal daily until it is successfully achieved.

THE POWER OF YOUR MAGNETIC ENERGY FIELD

Example: From Frustration to Delight in Just Thirty Days

Jeff, who was wanting to branch out in his career, had been sending out resumés, and going on interviews for more than a year with no positive results.

Since this was not working, he decided to switch from the methods he had been using to focusing on the desired end results. (Switching from the left-brain approach of problem solving to the right-brain approach.) He asked himself, "If I could have anything I wanted in a career, what would that be? In what kind of city would I be living? What qualities would I have in my life?"

This is the list he complied.

1. I'd have the ability to work anywhere in the U.S. at the drop of a hat.
2. I'd have a business of my own, with the option of people working for me, or I'd manage someone else's business, and get overrides on the production of others.
3. I'd have an income of $ _____ (a specific amount was written here).
4. I'd set my own working hours.
5. I'd be dressed professionally much of the time.
6. I'd make a difference in people's lives, and help them grow.
7. I'd enjoy time with happy, successful people.
8. I'd live in a warmer climate where winter clothing is rarely needed.
9. There would be flowers outside much of the year and trees that stayed green all year long.
10. I'd have the ease of getting around that's available in a small town along with the entertainment and business opportunities of a large, metropolitan city.
11. I'd be able to drive around and see different places and people.

Next, Jeff wrote his list in story form as if it had already happened. (Example: I am happy that I now have an income of $ _____ or more each month. I am thrilled that I am now living in a climate where I don't have to wear winter clothing . . . etc.)

He also made a tangible picture representing his end result to go along with the affirmations. Each day, he read the story and looked at the picture. He imagined being dressed professionally while helping happy, successful people become even more successful. He imagined the delight of looking at greenery all year long. He saw himself living in a climate where he didn't have to wear winter clothing. He felt the excitement of being able to work anywhere in the nation. He saw his bank statements showing his increased income each month.

Jeff also read accounts of people who had overcome great

obstacles. He thrilled to stories of people who had experienced miraculous answers to difficult situations. These stories helped to strengthen his belief that he could get what he wanted, and also increased the power of his magnetic energy field. Remember, he had been working on this goal for over a year with no positive results!

Less than thirty days after he had imagined enjoying his new life, he noticed an ad for a free tape along with information about the company's business opportunity. As he sent for the tape, he heard thoughts from his logical mind of, "Don't send for that. You already have that tape and have used it many times. You are taking advantage of them. You won't use it. You're getting something for nothing that you don't even need." However, he didn't let these thoughts stop him.

After receiving the tape, the company called him about their business opportunity. He was pleased to find that it met the requirements of every item on his list. He went on to be happy and successful in this new business.

Jeff's story demonstrates the steps you need to follow in creating your magnetic energy field. Once it is created, you are easily and quickly connected with what you need to achieve your goal.

1. Jeff used his left brain to decide exactly what he wanted in a career.
2. He dissolved negative thoughts and feelings from his subconscious.
3. He used the end-result principle to determine additional guidelines for his career, and made a tangible picture of his desired result.
4. He visualized the end result with feeling.
5. He read positive-thinking material, and specifically focused on people who had overcome obstacles to successfully reach their goals.
6. He listened to his right-brain hunches, and followed through on them, while continuing to do logical activities to reach his goal.

> ***By using the methods outlined in* The Secrets Of SuperSelling, *Jeff achieved in less than thirty days what he had previously been unable to do in over a year.***

Example: Seventeen Hundred to Zero

Janet was a successful real estate agent who had been a million-dollar producer five years in a row. Although she knew she had the ability to sell even more, she limited her production so she could devote a good bit of time to her husband and home.

Janet's life went along well until her marriage began to fall apart. She soon found herself in the middle of divorce proceedings and felt like a total failure. In addition to her personal problems, she also experienced a drastic drop in sales.

To deal with the drop in sales, Janet got busy doing the same activities she had done so successfully for the previous five years. Over a three-month period, she sent out 800 letters to homeowners offering a free market analysis. She called 600 people on the telephone asking if they would like to sell their homes. Finally, she personally knocked on 300 doors in an attempt to get listings. As incredible as it may seem, Janet did not get a single listing from all this activity!

The problems Janet was experiencing in her sales, along with her personal problems, caused her to seek help. She discovered the negative thoughts she had about herself, coupled with her unconscious belief that she didn't deserve listings and sales because she had "failed" as a wife. This created a negative magnetic energy field that pushed away from her the very sales she worked so hard to get!

While Janet had a positive goal of listing and selling properties, she also had an unconsciously-created negative goal of failing at real estate as she had failed at marriage. Since there was more feeling energy behind the negative goal of failing, her subconscious had to produce that result in her life.

This experience demonstrates the power of your magnetic energy field to push away from you anything different from the dominant thought and picture in your subconscious. Although Janet did the same activities that had produced sales for her in the past, she couldn't get a single listing from 1,700 attempts!

The good news is that Janet dissolved the negative goal, got her business and personal life back on track, and is once again selling successfully.

Remember, when there is a conflict, your subconscious acts on the belief behind which there is the most energy.

Example: Disbelief Decreases Sale

Henry has a wood-working business. One day he sold a man $90,000 worth of doors for his new home. Henry was jubilant over the sale, but also in a state of shock and disbelief that anyone would spend $90,000 on doors for his home. He even exclaimed to his wife, "I can't believe he would spend $90,000 on doors." Henry's wife was just as incredulous as he was. She called her friends and repeated, "We just can't believe anyone would spend $90,000 on doors!"

It wasn't long before the man called to say, "My father has convinced me I shouldn't spend more than $55,000 on the doors. We need to get together to redesign the project to fit into a $55,000 budget."

W. Clement Stone, founder of *Success* magazine said, "Most sales are made because of the way the salesman, not the prospect, thinks and acts." We might also say sales are lost because of the way the salesman, not the prospect, thinks and acts.

Henry conceived the sale, but since he couldn't believe the picture in his subconscious of $90,000 worth of doors for one home, his magnetic energy field had to push that result away from him.

Where thought goes, energy flows. People are influenced by the energy of your thoughts, even though they may be physically far away from you. If Henry had understood how his subconscious worked, he could have dissolved that disbelief from his mind, thereby saving the $90,000 sale.

Be sure to tell things the way you want them to be, for they are going to be the way you tell them.

NEGATIVE MAGNETIC ENERGY FIELDS

It is exciting to think of your positive magnetic energy field bringing you what you desire. However, it is equally important to understand how negative magnetic energy fields work. As you can see from the preceeding two stories, they are very powerful and can bring you what you don't want and push away from you the goals for which you strive so diligently.

One way negative magnetic energy fields are created is by making judgments. The dictionary defines the word judgment as follows:

1. A formal utterance of an authoritative opinion.
2. The process of forming an opinion or evaluation by discerning or comparing.

Characteristics of Judgments

Judgments can be both negative and positive. Whether they are negative or positive, they keep your energy stuck in the pattern formed by the judgments. They exist long after the original situation in which they were made disappears. Judgments keep coming back to your mind over and over because they are stuck in your magnetic energy field.

Judgmental actions, words, and feelings take the situation presently being judged, and project it into the future. You can be sure that anything you are being judgmental about right now is going to be a part of your life again in the future!

Judgments Can Have Detrimental Effects on Sales

Since judgments keep your energy locked in the pattern of the judgment, declaring that you are *not* doing as well as Jim or Tracy insures that you *don't* do as well. This has a detrimental effect on sales as do the statements in the following examples:

Examples of Negative Judgments

1. I can't close top executives, I just freeze up.
2. I'm not doing as well as I did last year, because the interest rates are up.
3. I just can't find the right job.
4. There is always a problem with that shipping company!
5. It takes three to six months to make your first sale in this business.
6. He hasn't been selling long enough to handle that big an account.
7. No matter what I say or do, they just don't reach their quota!
8. It's impossible to get good help.
9. I can't get any good salespeople!
10. They're just not following the program!

You may be thinking that some of the statements listed are simple facts about what is true at the moment. They can be just that. However, if you add enough feeling energy to the statement that it becomes a "formal utterance of an authoritative opinion," the statement changes from a simple observation to a judgment.

A statement becomes a judgment when it ceases being simply a description of a situation and becomes a definite opinion about the situation coupled with strong feelings.

HOW NEGATIVE JUDGMENTS HAPPEN

Step One: Something Happens That You Classify as Negative

When a customer brings back something they just bought, you have lost a sale and a commission or profit. You consider the customer bringing the item back to be a negative experience because you have lost money and must restock the merchandise.

Step Two: You Form Opinions About the Experience

From this experience, you may decide that the customer did something wrong, or that you failed to do something right. A feeling of anger or resentment then comes over you toward yourself, the other person, and the situation. You may be mad at yourself for not having done a better job of selling. You may be mad about the item being returned, and you may be angry at the customer for bringing it back. You may be resentful about having to restock the merchandise or do the extra paperwork. As a result of this, you may make the following judgments:

- "Customers are a nuisance."
- "Customers can't make up their minds. They don't know what they want!"
- "Half of what they buy during the holidays always comes back."
- "Credit card sales are such a hassle . . . half of them get returned, and you have all that extra paperwork for nothing!"

Along with anger and resentment, there may be a desire to have the other person feel as bad as you do or even worse. You want to punish the other person for what happened so that the offender feels the same bad feelings that you feel as a result of the merchandise being returned. Punishment is necessary in order for you to feel good once again.

THE EFFECT OF NEGATIVE JUDGMENTS ON AN ENERGY LEVEL

As you look at this situation in terms of energy and feelings, you will see why it hurts you when you make negative judgments and have negative feelings about yourself, another person, or a situation. The energy process is as follows:

1. You think angry thoughts about the situation.
   (The ⟍⟍ represents your negative feelings.)
2. You blame the offender. Blaming the offender (or yourself) increases the amount of negative energy within your system.
3. The offender receives the negative energy. He or she may not consciously realize anything is going on. However, on an energy level, your negative feelings are felt.
4. The offender blames you for your attitude about the return of the merchandise. Blaming you once again increases the amount of negative energy.
5. You receive the negative energy.
6. At this point, one of two things happens. You either continue to feel angry which increases the negative feelings, or you feel guilty for having been angry and try to make excuses for the offender. Continuing to feel angry or feeling guilty and trying to justify why the person returned the merchandise once again increases your negative energy.

7. You now go to a friend or co-worker and complain about the customer returning the item. The co-worker sympathizes and tells you about the same thing happening to him or her twice that week. You now spend some time talking about how awful it is. Talking with someone who agrees that this is awful increases the negative energy in your magnetic energy field.

8. Now you try to figure out what to do to replace this sale you've just lost. Trying to figure out what to do is not the same as tapping into your creativity. "Trying to figure out what to do" increases the negative energy even more.

Remember, like (energy) attracts like (energy). If you continue to hold pictures in your imagination of people returning merchandise, customers who return merchandise will be drawn to you. Since the amount of energy focused on returned merchandise has been increased through the process of blaming, justifying, getting sympathy, and trying to figure out what to do differently, you will increase the number of people buying things and returning them.

You can substitute any situation for "merchandise being returned." Here are just a few:

- Person says, "I'll be back," then doesn't return.
- Person acts like a sure sale and backs out at the last minute.
- Person meets with you an excessive number of times before buying.
- You fail to meet your quota.
- You hire a person who looks like he or she will be a superstar, but who doesn't produce as you expected.

*Remember, judgments exist long after the original
situation in which they were made is over.
They affect your sales and your life over and over,
because they are stuck in your magnetic
energy field.*

Example: "No Show"—Four In A Row Marcie is a sales person on commission. She calls people on the telephone, sets appointments, and meets with them at their homes or offices.

When she was new in sales and new in the area, she had a hard time prospecting. When she set appointments, she was delighted, and naturally hoped to make a sale.

One day she went on a sales call, and the person was not there. Marcie was very annoyed, for she had a strong sense of right and wrong. In her value system, it was right to be there, and wrong to stand someone up. In addition to being annoyed, she was disappointed that she didn't get the chance to give her sales presentation.

Marcie was very critical of herself for having set an appointment with someone who stood her up. She was also fearful about this happening again. She thought, "I don't understand, this person sounded so interested. She definitely seemed more interested than the person I scheduled for tomorrow. I wonder if tomorrow's appointment will show up? I sure can't sell someone who isn't there!"

You can probably guess what happened next. Three more appointments were "no shows." This made a total of four appointments in a row with no one there when she arrived. Marcie's energy was now vibrating in this "no show" pattern. Her thoughts were, "I'm there, I'm stood up and I'm mad, scared, and disappointed." From attending a Secrets Workshop, she remembered she needed to let go of the judgments and the accompanying fears. She forgave herself along with the four people who stood her up and declared, "I no longer set appointments with people who don't keep them. Everyone keeps their appointments with me." This allowed her to get on with her selling.

Negative Judgments Prevent You From Learning New Skills

Let's focus for a minute on the judgment, "I can't close top executives." When the energy in your magnetic energy field is locked into this form, it keeps vibrating to the tune of, "I can't close top executives." Your subconscious is then locked into leading you to top executives whom you can't close. You are also prohibited from learning and applying new sales skills that would help you improve your closing average. If a sales manager, colleague, or friend suggests a training course or a new way to close, you can't take advantage of the information. It is not that you are stubborn. Your energy field absolutely prohibits you from doing what's needed to make it possible for you to close top executives, until you dissolve the judgment.

You might make the judgment that you can't close top executives based on the fact that you're new in the business, or don't know the product well enough, etc. Later on when those facts change, you are still stuck with the judgments even though the condition that brought them on in the first place no longer exists.

Situations about which you are holding negative judgments will happen over and over again. In addition, they'll get worse unless you become aware of your judgments and dissolve them.

Judgments May Be Kept From Your Conscious Mind Through Denial

You may make judgments without being consciously aware of doing so. They are kept from your conscious mind through the process of denial. The following definitions of "denial" relate to judgments:

1. The refusal to satisfy a request or desire.
2. The refusal to admit the truth of a statement or charge.
3. The refusal to acknowledge a person or thing.

You may be mad about not reaching your sales goals, and make some judgments about your business or yourself. You then refuse to acknowledge these judgments and feelings. You may also refuse to acknowledge your feelings and/or refuse to grant your requests:

1. You refuse to admit how mad you are.
2. You refuse to admit how disappointed you are.
3. You refuse to stop beating on yourself about your mistakes.
4. You refuse to let yourself have that much money in one day (month, year.)
5. You refuse to let yourself have what you really want and settle for less.

You may wonder how you can set a goal, and at the same time refuse to allow yourself to reach that goal. An understanding of Ego States clears up this confusion. According to transactional analysis, developed by Eric Berne, there are three ego states within us. These ego states each function in a unique way. Your Parent ego state sets limits for you based on your values and beliefs. Your Adult ego state deals with facts and figures, and is logical. Your Child ego state is curious, determined, funny, spontaneous, and creative. It controls 45 percent of your energy and responds to life very much like little children do. (For a more thorough explanation of transactional analysis, see Secret Nine.)

Each ego state can make a different decision. There may have been times when the following has happened:

a. Your Parent has refused to grant requests from your Child.
b. Your Child has refused to grant requests from your Parent.
c. Your Adult has refused to learn what was needed to achieve a goal desired by either your Parent or your Child.
d. Your Parent has refused to acknowledge that your Child was even there trying to get permission to satisfy a desire.

Remember, your Child needs your Parent's permission to do whatever is desired. When your Parent refuses to even acknowledge that your Child is there, it is the same as the boss of your company being in his or her office with the thick wooden door closed and locked. The boss won't come out and you can't get in. You stand waiting and waiting to no avail.

   e. Your Child has refused to acknowledge that your Parent was even there. Your Child is in its own room with the thick door closed and locked. It won't come out and you can't get in. You stand waiting and waiting to no avail.

The situations presented in (a), (b), and (c) frequently result in anger and resentment. The situations in (d) and (e) often result in feelings of hopelessness. You feel powerless to change the situation and may resign yourself to living the rest of your life in the status quo.

The point here is that there have been many times in your life when you have run up against the roadblock of one of your ego states absolutely refusing to agree to go along with what you want or worse yet, refusing to even listen to your request.

Your Child ego state may have a desire to be the top salesperson in your company. Your Parent ego state may have absorbed the belief that, "salespeople are cheats and liars." Based on this latter belief, your Parent will respond to your Child by refusing to grant your request to be the top salesperson. It may not want you to be a salesperson at all!

If your Child overrides your Parent, and you get into sales anyway, your Parent may refuse to acknowledge that you are selling. If you sell computers, your Parent may describe your occupation as "demonstrating machines to companies" rather than "selling computers."

On the other hand, your Parent may have a burning desire for you to be a top-notch salesperson. Your Child may have a problem with selling, and refuse to be a successful salesperson.

Denials by themselves are neither negative nor positive. The way they are used determines their classification. In the instances just mentioned, one ego state mentions a desire to sell and the other refuses to go along with the idea. Since these refusals hold you back from getting what you want, they are classified as negative denials. The denials mentioned in Secret Two, such as refusing to acknowledge the commonly-held belief that you get a cold when you go outside with a wet head or gain weight from eating, create a positive result for you and are therefore called positive denials.

- Negative denials are held in place in your magnetic energy field with judgments, emotional control, and suppression of feelings.
- The combination of negative denials and judgments together prevent you from dissolving unwanted energy patterns. As you refuse to acknowledge your judgments and feelings, you are trapped in the patterns created by the judgments.

As these situations pile up, your resentment level and your feeling of hopelessness increase as well. However, it is possible to clear this accumulated energy from your system. (To do this, see Activities For Dissolving Energy Blocks in Secret Ten.)

The Negative Effect of Positive Judgments

Judgments can "sound good" and "appear" to have a positive effect on sales. When you declare with feeling that you are doubling your income, or that you are meeting your sales quota with ease, your energy is formed into that positive pattern. Your energy field must then draw to you the right conditions for you to double your income or meet your quota with ease. Judgments can be uttered by your sales manager, family or friends, or can be declared by you about yourself.

Although judgments are comfortable for some people, there is a negative side to positive judgments. Some salespeople seem driven by their goal to be number one or to do better each year regardless of what is happening in their lives at the present time. The driven quality comes from the fact that judgments lock your energy into that pattern, and you're not free to do anything different.

When your goal to be number one or to do better than you did last year becomes a judgment, you really don't have a choice about the amount of time you spend in your business. You are locked into working long hours, and your work is done compulsively, rather than by choice.

Examples of Positive Judgments

1. He's the best salesman I've got!
2. She always makes her quota.

3. You can count on them to deliver on the date they promise.
4. I double my income every year!
5. I win all the contests hands down!
6. I just love to close.

HOW POSITIVE JUDGMENTS HAPPEN

Step One: Something Happens That You Classify as Positive.

You get an award for being the top salesperson for the year and feel really good about yourself.

Step Two: You Form Opinions About the Experience.

You may decide that being number-one is the only way to play the game. Because of the attention you get, the respect you receive, and your own increased self esteem, you make the following statements:

- "This is the only way to go!"
- "I'm going to be number-one again and again and again!"
- "I don't care what it takes . . . nobody is taking this award away from me next year!"

Along with the positive judgments, you feel proud, happy, and excited. You also feel a great commitment to your goal of being number-one again and again. As was stated earlier, the negative effect of positive judgments is that you don't have a choice about the amount of time and effort you put into achieving your goals. You attack your work with a driven quality.

Before we cover the steps involved in freeing yourself from all judgments, both positive and negative, and the benefits to be gained, let's briefly review the process of making judgments.

A Review of the Process of Making Judgments

1. You have an experience and react to it with strong opinions and intense feelings.
2. You have now locked your energy into that pattern. You then react to the experience *plus* your judgment of it.
3. You control your feelings. You don't express them, and if it is a negative experience, you try to "put on a happy face."
4. Your controlled feelings keep the energy vibrating in the pattern determined by judgments.
5. You then keep getting more of the same situations until you dissolve the judgments.

Freedom From Judgments Gives You Freedom of Choice

If you are free from all judgments, both positive and negative, your energy field can be molded each month into whatever income level you choose. In September you can choose, "I am creating a $5,000 income this month." October's goal can be, "I am creating a $7,500 income this month." In November you may decide, "I am taking this month off." After your rest, you jump in with a goal for December of "I am creating an income of $12,000 this month!"

Example: One of the authors' clients who was a mortgage loan originator decided each month's income in just this way. He gave himself time deadlines for reaching each goal and celebrated periodically with vacations.

When his income slipped, he found more things he really wanted which stimulated his desire to increase his production. In one thirty-day period, his income increased from $5,000 to $8,500 because he chose some new things that he really wanted to do with his money.

Freeing Yourself From All Judgments

As you review the process of making judgments, you see from step one that you can prevent judgments from happening by learning to stop reacting to situations with negative feelings. This doesn't mean that you become a zombie with no feelings—it means that you choose whether or not you will have feelings about a situation, and you choose what emotion you will feel. When you react, you are like a puppet whose strings are being pulled by someone else, and you are insured of getting more of the same.

The next step in freeing yourself from judgments is repeating the following permission statements daily along with your personal denials and affirmations:

1. I give myself permission to be successful.
2. I give myself permission to have exactly what I want.
3. I give myself permission to have as much as I want of any good thing.
4. I give myself permission to be happy.
5. I give myself permission to make noise.
6. I give myself permission to share my good feelings with others.
7. I give myself permission to feel good.
8. I give myself permission to be excited.
9. I give myself permission to stop refusing to grant my own requests.
10. I give myself permission to stop feeling sad, mad, or scared about not getting exactly what I want, and to get what I truly want.

As we have stated earlier, the Child within you does not do anything without the permission of the internal Parent. Therefore, it may be necessary for you to first give yourself permission to be, do, or have, before you state your denials and affirmations. Permission statements can be combined with positive denials and affirmations as follows:

113

- "I give myself permission to have exactly what I want. I no longer have to settle for second best. I get exactly what I say I am going to get!"
- "I give myself permission to stop refusing to grant my own requests and to stop feeling bad about not getting exactly what I want. I also give myself permission to have exactly what I want and to be salesperson of the month. It's not true that I don't do as well as Jim or Tracy. I do so well that I am salesperson of the month at least 50 percent of the year. I give myself permission to feel good, to be happy, and to share my good feelings with others."

Being free from judgments and consciously
creating your positive magnetic energy field
gives you the power to be, do, or have anything
you want!

CHECKING FOR UNDERSTANDING

Create Your Magnetic Energy Field

1. Everything in your life is first created in your imagination.   T   F

2. To get the result, you have to create an image in your imagination just like your tangible picture.   T   F

3. Your image in your imagination must be projected out into space to get the result you want as easily as possible.   T   F

4. Your feelings help project your internal image into space.   T   F

5. You must have a strong feeling connected to your visualization.   T   F

6. You never have to energize the picture of your goal in your imagination more than once.   T   F

7. Once a goal is accomplished, the magnetic energy field is dissolved.   T   F

8. Saying your affirmations out loud is an important part of developing your magnetic energy field.   T   F

9. Your magnetic energy field pulls to you what you have programmed into your subconscious and pushes away from you anything different.   T   F

10. Energy fields have never been photographed.   T   F

11. Judgments don't hold your energy in any particular pattern.   T   F

12. Judgments insure that what you are experiencing now gets repeated in the future.   T   F

Answers:

1. T	5. T	9. T
2. T	6. F	10. F
3. T	7. I	11. F
4. T	8. T	12. T

AVOIDING NEGATIVE ENERGY

Information: The amount of energy you have available to focus on your chosen goals makes a difference in whether you achieve your goals easily or with difficulty. Just as it is harder to push a car when you have only one or two people pushing it, it is harder to achieve a goal when your energy is weak and scattered.

Feeling fearful, angry, resentful, sad, or depressed sets up a negative energy field which brings you more of the same feelings. Negativity depletes your energy level leaving you very little to go on, just as leaving your car lights on overnight runs your car battery down. Therefore, it is important to do whatever you can to decrease the number of negative experiences in your life. The following questions are offered to help you identify Negative

Factors that drain your energy level, thereby making it harder for you to achieve your goals.

Directions: Negative Factors (If the answer to any question is yes, list the people, foods, or activities on a separate sheet of paper.) In situations involving you and someone else, share your thoughts and feelings in a win/win way by saying something like the following: "I am upset about the fact that you don't follow through on the agreements you make with me. It results in my wasting my time, and having difficulties getting things done according to my time schedule. I want you to keep any future agreements you make with me. Will you do that?"

1. Does anyone put you down? If so, whom? About what?
2. Is anyone jealous of you? If so, whom? About what?
3. Does anyone repeatedly invite you to feel guilty? If so, whom? About what?
4. Does anyone cut off your joy by changing the subject when you are excited about something? If so, whom?
5. Does anyone close to you bore you? If so, whom? Why?
6. Do any of your friends, colleagues, or business associates not follow through on agreements with you? If so, whom?
7. Are you angry at anyone? If so, whom? About what?

Directions: Negative Factors (If the answer to any question is yes, list the activities, foods, or people on a separate sheet of paper.) In situations involving just yourself, identify the problem and take action to correct it. Eliminating these negative factors increases your stamina and physical energy.

Examples: If you feel tired after eating certain foods, stop eating them. If you feel sad about not having reached your sales quota, identify the skill you need to work on and get additional training in prospecting or closing, etc. If some of your activities bore you but must be done, set a goal to increase your income so that you can hire that activity done.

1. Do any of the activities you do bore you? If so, what?
2. Do you feel tired after you eat certain foods? If so, which ones?

3. Do any of your activities (work or leisure) upset you (make you nervous, make your stomach tight, etc.)? If so, which ones?

4. Do you put yourself down? If so, about what?

5. Do you worry? If so, about what?

6. Are you resentful about anything? If so, about what?

7. Are you fearful of anyone or about anything? If so, who and/or what?

8. Are you sad? If so, about what?

9. Are you depressed? If so, about what?

INCREASING POSITIVE ENERGY

Information: The amount of energy you focus on your chosen goals makes a difference in how quickly and easily you achieve them. It is easier to achieve a goal when your energy is strong and focused.

Feeling happy, excited, joyful, proud and enthusiastic sets up a positive energy field, which brings you more of the same feelings. Positive feelings increase your stamina, and result in a feeling of well being. Studies have shown that people with serious illnesses improved after watching shows that caused them to laugh on a daily basis.

Directions: The following activity will help you identify some of the factors that can aid in energizing your goals.

Positive Factors: List the people, foods, or activities on a separate sheet of paper.

1. Who calms you if and when you are upset?

2. Who laughs with you?

3. Who recognizes your accomplishments, and enthuses with you?

4. Who supports you in thinking big?

5. Who confronts you if and when you're doing things that are either harmful or non-productive?

6. Who gives you what you ask for easily and joyfully?
7. Which friends pep you up?
8. What foods energize you?
9. What activities energize you?
10. What activities relax you?
11. For what do you compliment yourself?
12. What makes you laugh?

Once you have identified the people and activities that energize you positively and negatively, you may want to decrease the negative factors you have identified and increase the positive factors. As you increase the positive factors, the amount of energy available for you to use in achieving your personal dreams is increased tremendously.

REPELLING UNWANTED EXPERIENCES

Directions: It is possible to use your energy field to repel things that you don't want to experience. Since your energy field has to push away anything different from what is in your subconscious, you simply empty your subconscious of things you don't want in your life.

The first step is to identify what you want to eliminate.

On a separate sheet of paper, list the frustrations you experience in your selling. Here are a few examples:

1. People standing you up when you have an appointment.
2. People who want to buy your product or service, but can't get financing.
3. Inventory that doesn't arrive on time.
4. Other people holding up your deal, because they don't do their job on time.

5. Prospects who don't tell you the truth when they fill out an application; when the truth is finally known, the deal is lost.

The next step is to make a picture to represent the frustrations you have identified.

1. Get a picture of an office with no one sitting at the desk. Put your photograph on the same page showing that you are there and your prospect is not. Put an X on the picture and write, "No one stands me up anymore. My prospects are always there to meet with me and buy from me."

2. Get a picture of someone who looks very sad. Put it on the page and write, "REJECTED—BAD CREDIT." Draw an X on the page and write, "None of my prospects are rejected because of bad credit or other problems. I don't call on people who can't get financing anymore. All my prospects have good credit, or have enough cash for my product/service."

3. Get a picture of the place where you receive your inventory (post office, office, etc.). Put a photograph of you looking sad on the page. Draw a big X on the page and write, "I'm never disappointed because my inventory doesn't arrive on time. It's always here when I expect it."

4. Get a picture of the people who used to hold up your deals. Write on the page, "No one holds up my deals anymore. They do their jobs quickly and efficiently and everything works like clockwork."

5. Get one of your applications that was rejected and write on it in big letters, "REJECTED—PROSPECT DIDN'T TELL TRUTH ABOUT SOME ITEMS." Draw a big X on that one. Write on it, "None of my prospects get rejected because they lie on their applications." Get another application that was accepted. Write in big letters, "ACCEPTED." Write on it, "All my prospects tell the truth and are accepted."

The idea is to say that the unwanted behavior doesn't happen, and to follow it with the desired behavior. Look at the pictures daily. Remember, once an idea is altered in your subconscious, the result is altered. Once an idea is dissolved, you no longer have that result in your life.

By controlling your subconscious,
you control your life.

THE POWER OF NO

Information: Children are often prohibited from saying no to parents, school teachers, doctors, dentists, and other authority figures. Saying no to parents is often redefined by the parents as "talking back, being impudent and showing disrespect." Child development books have a section on "The Terrible Twos" in which they describe the behavior of the two year old whose major vocabulary is no. Saying no is effectively trained out of many children.

However, the ability to say no with vigor is a necessary part of putting a stop to conditions you no longer want in your life. Saying no to missing your quota is just as necessary as saying yes to reaching your quota. If you buy a wonderful new car but have an old one in your garage, you must remove it before you can drive the new one into the garage. Saying no to the unwanted condition is the same as removing the old car from the garage.

Saying no must be done with conviction. Remember, your subconscious acts on your most dominant thought. If you still feel bad about missing your quota while you are saying no to missing your quota, your subconscious is going to act on your most dominant thought. You want to be sure that your dominant thought is "No!" "No more missed quotas!"

Directions: To help you develop your ability to say no with conviction and to feel comfortable saying no, get a person to do the following exercise with you.

1. Think about a condition you want to dissolve from your life (example: cancelled orders) and the corresponding goal you want to achieve.

2. Sit facing each other as close as possible. Begin saying "no" over and over while your partner repeats "yes." Your no represents the whole idea of "no to missing quotas." Your partner's yes represents your continuing to miss your quotas.

3. Vary your tone of voice and your volume as you continue saying no and your partner keeps repeating yes. The idea is for each of you to be so strong in your energy and enthusiasm that the other person gives up.

4. Repeat the process until you say no with such conviction that your partner gives up.

Repeat this process until you feel very comfortable saying no with conviction. Remember to say no to negative conditions before you affirm the achievement of the positive goal.

IDENTIFYING AND DISSOLVING NEGATIVE DENIALS

Directions: On a separate sheet of paper, jot down ideas you come up with from reading the following questions. As you identify areas where you have refused to grant your own requests, or refused to acknowledge desires, talents or abilities, make a list of the items. You will use this list to create your own positive denials.

- What creative ideas do you have that you've cast aside as being "not good enough?"
- What sales targets have you avoided aiming for because you tell yourself you wouldn't be able to hit them?
- What production schedules have you not seriously considered because you already *know* they are impossible?
- What things are you refusing to allow yourself to have by insisting they are too expensive, and you could never earn enough to afford them?
- Are you refusing to acknowledge how good you really are at what you do?
- Are you refusing to admit you need training in a certain area?

- What do you want that you've not yet let yourself have? (Include clothes, vacations, awards, cars, houses, friends, ideal weight, time to read, the whole house straightened up at the same time, etc.)
- What feelings do you refuse to let yourself feel? (There is a difference between "knowing" you are mad, and "feeling" your anger. Do you "feel" love, joy, satisfaction, fear, etc.?)
- What talents do you have that you don't admit to having? This doesn't have to be something as spectacular as painting like the old masters. It may be as simple as brightening the day of most of the people you meet.
- What abilities aren't you using to their fullest?
- What compliments do you get that you don't believe about yourself? (Someone says, "You're a great closer." You think to yourself, "I miss two out of every four." If you do anything other than agree with the compliment, you are not believing that compliment . . . list those.)
- Are there things that are important to you that you try to pretend don't matter? (This might be things like, time to learn a foreign language, having your mate greet you at the door with a kiss, being one of the top salespeople with your company, being competent in some sport, having a garden, having your mate pay as much attention to you now as he or she did before the children arrived, etc.)

Directions: You can dissolve the negative situations you have been experiencing by creating positive denials. To do this, simply fill in the blanks with the information you gathered from the preceeding questions.

1. It is not true that_____.
2. I no longer believe_____.
3. I am not_____.

Follow each denial with an affirmation that states the result as you want it to be.

Examples:

1. "It is not true that I can't be salesperson of the month because I'm not a good enough closer. I'm a great closer."

2. "I no longer believe I can't close top executives. I'm great at closing top executives."

3. "I no longer believe I can't find employees who will do a good job. I find competent employees easily."

4. "I no longer believe I can't earn enough to afford the things I really want. I can earn any amount of money I want by reaching my sales goals."

Repeat the positive denials daily until you no longer experience the negative results. You may read and write them, or record them on a cassette tape which you play each day.

IDENTIFYING NEGATIVE JUDGMENTS

Directions: On a separate sheet of paper, do the following activities to help you identify and dissolve negative judgments from your subconscious.

1. List any deals that have fallen through during your career.

2. List any situations you wish you had done differently.

3. Describe any recurring situation that happens in your life you don't like. This may be in any area of your life. (Use the John James Game Plan in Secret Nine to do this.)

4. Finish the following statements:

   a. Customers are_____.

   b. Bosses are_____.

   c. Friends are_____.

   d. Customers, (bosses, colleagues, etc.) ought to be___.

   e. Parents (children, relatives, etc.) ought to be_____.

   f. The economy_____.

   g. I hate it when_____.

   h. If only the company (boss, customer, wife, husband, son, daughter, etc.) would_____.

Once you have identified your judgments, clear them from your subconscious with positive denials.

IDENTIFYING AND DISSOLVING FEAR

Information: Feelings catapult your internal images out into the atmosphere so that your magnetic energy field can pull to you what is pictured in your imagination and push away from you anything different from your internal pictures. It doesn't matter whether you feel a desire to reach your goals, or feel fear that you will not reach them. Both emotions have equal power to pull to you the image attached to the feeling. Fear catapults your internal image of not reaching your goal just as desire catapults your internal image of success.

Directions: Take inventory of your fears related to success, money, recognition, and responsibility. The following questions will help you start the ball rolling. Add any additional fears of which you are aware.

1. What fears do you have related to becoming more prosperous?

- Do you worry your friends and relatives will be jealous?
- Might your friends and relatives expect you to always pay the check?
- Are you afraid they will be asking you for loans?
- Do you dread the additional responsibilities of more bank accounts and investments, etc.?
- Are you afraid you will be robbed?

2. What fears do you have related to getting more recognition?

- Will your co-workers be asking you to spend much of your time teaching them what you know?
- Are you afraid you will lose some of your privacy?

- Are you afraid people will expect you to achieve to an even higher level?

3. What fears do you have related to becoming more successful?

- Will you have less free time?
- Will you have more responsibility?
- Will you need a support staff to manage your business?
- Are you afraid you will get "the fever" and never again be satisfied with the status quo?

4. What fears do you have related to not being successful in sales or sales management?

- Are you afraid you will be embarrassed or ashamed with your friends and family?
- Do you fear having to get a "regular job" with a ceiling on your income?
- Do you fear letting the company or your family down?

Directions: Dissolve the fears by creating positive denials. To do this, simply fill in the blanks with the information you gathered from the preceeding questions.

1. I'm not afraid that _____.
2. I no longer fear_____.
3. I am not worried that_____.

Follow each denial with an affirmation that states the result as you want it to be.

Example:

1. "I'm not afraid that I won't be salesperson of the month because I'm not a good enough closer. I'm a great closer."

Repeat the positive denials and affirmations daily until you no longer experience the negative results. You may read and write them, or record them on a cassette tape which you play each day.

Directions: You may also want to dissolve your fears by visualizing the positive achievement of your goals as well as repeating the positive denials and affirmations. Use The Art of Dissolving in Secret Five to deal with your fears on an energy level.

POSITIVE AFFIRMATIONS

Directions: Repeat these affirmations on a daily basis to internalize the principles of your subconscious, and hasten the achievement of your desired results.

1. I easily dissolve all limiting judgments from my thoughts and energy field.
2. Because I don't hold judgments, I am free to set new goals as needed.
3. Each time I set a new goal, I excitedly create a magnetic energy field for that goal.
4. I increase the power of my energy field by eating a well-balanced diet and getting plenty of rest.
5. It's fun to energize my goals on a regular basis until they are achieved.
6. I have strong positive feelings about my goals.
7. I enjoy taking time to enthuse about my successes on a daily basis.
8. I schedule time to celebrate and rest after major accomplishments.
9. I feel confident that I can repeat my successes on a regular basis.

THE
SECRETS
OF
SUPERSELLING

Secret Five

Avoid Negative Programming

PREVIEW OF SECRET FIVE

AVOID NEGATIVE PROGRAMMING

In Secret Five you learn how you may unconsciously create negative goals from your own thoughts, conversations with other people, or from what you see, hear, or read in the media. You discover that mistakes are sometimes the way our subconscious realizes your unconsciously created goals. You read stories of salespeople who unconsciously created negative goals which blocked their sales, and how they overcame the blocks.

AVOID NEGATIVE PROGRAMMING

UNCONSCIOUSLY CREATED GOALS

At times things happen to you that seem like accidents, mistakes, or the result of circumstances. This may not always be the case. These experiences may actually be the result of unconsciously created goals that have been programmed into your subconscious without your realizing it. They are created from intense wishes, thoughts, frustrations, or desires. Let's look at an example of an unconsciously created goal.

Example: Henry and his wife, Joan, drove to a conference where Joan was scheduled to speak. When they arrived at their destination, Henry discovered that Joan's luggage had been left behind. It appeared that Henry had "forgotten" to put hers in although he had remembered his own.

Since there wasn't time to return home for the luggage before her scheduled speech, Joan went to a store and purchased the clothing she needed as a speaker for the conference.

On the surface, it appears as though Henry is either inconsiderate, or a forgetful person. This is not so. The truth is, Henry had been wanting Joan to buy new clothes for some time, and hadn't been able to get her to purchase anything. While he didn't consciously leave her luggage in order to force her to buy new clothing, unconsciously it was another story.

Here are the thoughts that went into Henry's subconscious:

1. I want Joan to have some new clothes, but don't know how to get her to purchase them.

2. Joan feels guilty about buying new clothes when she feels she doesn't absolutely need them.

3. I want Joan to look especially good when she speaks at a conference.

The job of your subconscious is to find a way to produce the result(s) you desire using all the available data.

By leaving her luggage at home, Henry created a situation whereby Joan really needed the clothing she purchased. This did away with any guilt she might have felt about getting new clothes.

If Henry had focused on his inability to get Joan to buy some new clothes, and felt the frustration of her not wanting to get them, his subconscious would have produced the result of Joan not getting new clothes. However, his desire to have her buy the clothes was so strong, he unconsciously facilitated the purchase of new clothes by leaving Joan's luggage at home.

Henry didn't realize he was creating the mishap. He did not sit down and write out an action plan for getting new clothes for Joan. He simply had thoughts and feelings over a period of time that were intense enough to reach his subconscious, and the desired result was produced in a way that was a complete surprise.

As we've said before, your subconscious is working twenty-four hours a day, seven days a week, to make your pictures, thoughts, and feelings real.

Pictures, thoughts, and feelings that are repeated over and over get accepted by your subconscious as goals to be achieved.

CREATING UNCONSCIOUS NEGATIVE GOALS

The following example shows how a negative goal was unconsciously created in someone's sales career.

Example: Frank became one of the top sales professionals in the country with his company, and attended a dinner honoring the top salespeople. After the festivities were over, Frank began to worry about how he would live up to the achievement level he had set. He began to feel pressured by the weight of servicing present accounts while prospecting for and selling new accounts.

A short time later, Frank started having trouble with his sales. He would make a sale, and the very next day the person would return the merchandise, and cancel the contract. He would sell to someone else who would want to keep the merchandise, but could not get accepted by the financing company. He realized that if present conditions continued, he would soon be out of business.

Consciously he wanted to stay in business. However, because of his fear of not being able to maintain his recent level of production while servicing his accounts, he also had created an unconscious negative goal to get out of business.

In talking with his sales manager about his situation, he learned he had set unrealistic expectations for himself that resulted in his unconsciously wanting to leave the business. Once he realized this, he programmed his subconscious positively. His sales then went back to normal.

Let's look now at an example of how unconsciously created negative goals block sales.

Example: Barbara is a real estate agent who had a property that had been on the market for several months. She was doing the following activities to sell the house:

1. Sending out flyers to advertise the property.
2. Putting ads in the newspaper.
3. Holding an open house on weekends.
4. Placing the house on the caravan list so other agents would go through the property.
5. Calling former customers and asking if they knew anyone who was interested in buying a house.

Barbara was at her wits' end. She felt she couldn't work any harder marketing this property than she already was. She was also concerned because the listing would expire in two weeks. She feared the owners might then list the house with another company, and all her hard work would be wasted.

As Barbara went about the process of marketing the house, she kept thinking the following thoughts:

1. The house has been on the market four months.
2. There have been no offers made on the house.
3. There are no likely prospects in sight.
4. The owners must sell soon.
5. The listing will expire in two weeks, and the owners may list with another company.

This assessment caused her to become worried and afraid. She was frustrated at not knowing what to do, and was also angry that she hadn't come up with an idea that worked. Since she had gone so long with no offers, she was doubting whether she could do in the next two weeks what she had been unable to do in the previous four months. Through repetition of pictures, thoughts, and feelings, Barbara's subconscious accepted the description of what was true at the moment (which was not what she wanted) as the result she wanted produced.

Barbara's Unconscious Negative Goals

1. No offers
2. No likely prospects
3. House doesn't sell
4. Listing expires and is lost
5. Don't get paid

Remember, your subconscious does not evaluate or judge. It cannot tell the difference between a description of the way things are at the moment, and the goal you have set. It accepts anything you repeat with feeling as a goal to be achieved.

While Barbara was busy working, her subconscious was busy making sure there were no offers, and no likely prospects in sight so the listing could expire before the property was sold.

At the last moment, Barbara consulted with one of the authors about what she might do to make the sale. After she was helped to understand what was happening, she was told to declare: "This house is selling while it is my listing, and I'm getting paid for my work."

Next, she was told to go through the house visualizing it as sold. She wrote "SOLD on or before Jan. 12" across one of the fliers used to market the property. The idea of the house being sold on time now became her dominant thought. Her subconscious then had to produce the result of the house being sold in the required time frame, because Barbara accepted this as being accomplished. She didn't worry about how it was to be done. She was already doing the usual work to sell properties. She simply allowed her dominant thought to be, "The house is sold."

As she relaxed, her confidence in the sale grew, and a creative idea for marketing the property suddenly came to her. She thought of walking the neighborhood and asking the neighbors if they knew anyone who would like to buy the house. One of the neighbors who lived a few blocks away had not noticed that the house was for sale. She was excited when Barbara told her about the house being available because her brother was moving to that city soon and hoped to buy in that area.

The house was sold two days later to the neighbor's brother.

IT'S EVERYWHERE . . . IT'S EVERYWHERE

As you have learned in the previous section, your subconscious can be programmed negatively without your being consciously aware of it. In the following section, you will look at a number of ways unconscious programming occurs during your everyday activities.

Negative Programming and the Media

As you relax and listen to popular music, you often react to the words and sounds with feelings. If you hear the same song day after day, the lyrics as well as your feelings about them will be programmed into your subconscious. If the words tell a positive story, you are programming yourself positively. If they tell a negative story, you are programming yourself negatively. If you continually listen to songs that tell of a wonderful love that went sour with the couple finally breaking up, do not be surprised if your own relationship breaks up. If you repeatedly hear about a person who hates his or her job, do not be surprised if this happens to you in your job.

Popular music is not the only thing that may be negatively programming you without your being aware of it. As you watch television, you see images and hear messages that cause you to react with feelings. Television is a powerful source of programming for your subconscious, because it combines visual and auditory impact.

If you watch a program that is on daily, and the characters in the program are always unhappy with each other or dealing with some kind of crisis, you may begin having those same experiences in your life.

Maybe the characters you watch on a regular basis make you laugh and you think laughter is therapeutic. It is true that laughter does heal. However, if the character makes you laugh by playing the buffoon, or by always messing up, you may be programming yourself to play the buffoon, or mess up and accept this behavior as funny. Correcting the things you mess up is no fun. It wastes much time and energy that could be used to create new things you want in your life.

Remember, programs that you see and/or hear regularly about people who are sad, frightened, or angry are programming you to feel those same emotions.

Signs are another source of negative programming. We see them in homes, offices, stores, and on car bumpers. While they may be amusing for a moment, repeatedly reading them programs your subconscious to produce the result they express. For example, if you frequently read, "Whatever can go wrong will," your subconscious works twenty-four hours a day, non-stop, to make this saying true in your life. In this way, the messages become self-fulfilling prophecies.

While it is important to stay informed by reading the newspaper or watching the news on television, there are also negative aspects involved in these activities.

Starting your day off by listening to the news may generate feelings of hopelessness, sadness, or fear as you listen to murders, kidnappings, accidents, and such. Ending your day by watching the late news likewise can generate negative feelings just as you are about to go to sleep. Since your subconscious is most accessible as you are waking and before sleeping, you want to program it positively at these times.

If you doubt the power of radio, television, movies, videos, cassettes, compact discs, newspapers, magazines, and signs, you might want to try the following experiment. For a week watch and listen only to programs that are frightening, sad, angry, etc. Then be aware of your daily thoughts and feelings.

For the next week, watch and listen only to programs that deal with happiness, success, and accomplishment. Be aware of your thoughts and feelings during this time also. See for yourself if there is a difference in the way you think and feel, and in the results you achieve. (To get a stronger feeling for how negative and positive programming play a part in your life, try the experiment for a longer period of time.)

Negative Programming and Other People

In addition to the negative programming you receive through the media, it is important to be aware of your interactions with the people around you. Be aware of their conversations. Are they predominantly positive? Do they talk of success, fun, and happiness? Are their conversations mainly negative? Do they dote on illness, having too little love, too many bills, not enough money, or a boss or job they don't like? As the people around you talk, their feelings flow over you just like water pouring over a waterfall. These feelings affect you, and you either find yourself feeling the same as they do, or you exert considerable energy to keep yourself from taking on their feelings.

It is important that you monitor what you say to yourself and others. If you have things going on in your life that are not what you want, it is crucial that you do not keep telling your friends and yourself how things are now.

If something happened in the past that you didn't like, don't keep talking and thinking about it. When you do this, you are guaranteeing more of the same by programming the past into your present. If you say something often enough for it to be firm in your mind, you have created an affirmation. If you repeat the affirmation enough, it becomes a self-fulfilling prophecy. Examples of this are statements such as, "I never remember people's names," or "I can never find things when I want them!"

If you want to program your mind and body with positive energy, you may want to stay away from people and media that are negative. It is tremendously helpful to have friends and outside influences who are uplifting sources of positive programming and energy.

> *Let go of the past, be in the present
> and consciously create your future.*

THE ART OF DISSOLVING

There are times when it is not possible or appropriate to stay away from people who are negative. Sales managers frequently have to deal with salespeople who are feeling down about not having reached their sales targets. Salespeople sometimes have to handle the complaints of customers and prospects. They may also have disturbing situations in their personal lives with which to cope.

The art of dissolving is a process you can use to clear up negativity in minutes. It can be used to dissolve your own (or others) negative feelings and judgments so that they do not get repeated.

As you learned in Secret Four, negative energy is increased when the following occurs:

1. Something negative happens and people experience negative emotions. (Represented by the circle.)

2. Next, they blame themselves or someone else for what

happened. This increases the quantity of negative energy.

3. They then find reasons to excuse the behavior that caused the situation. This again increases the quantity of negative energy.

4. By now they are feeling pretty bad, and they look for friends who will sympathize with them. As others agree with them about how awful it is or how irresponsible the other person is, the negative energy is once again increased.

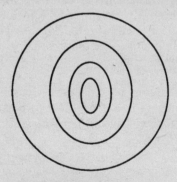

5. Now they try to figure out how to fix the problem or deal with the situation. Trying to figure out how to fix the problem on top of the negative emotions already existing once again increases the amount of negative energy.

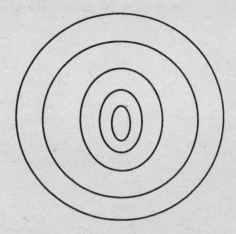

6. When no solution is found, they experience frustration, fear, or anger, and blame themselves or others. This increases the amount of negative energy. They then find reasons for not being able to find a solution which once again increases the negative energy. The cycle keeps repeating itself.

Often people think that what the person wants or needs most is advice on how to handle the situation. This is not so. People can often figure out how to handle situations. What they need before they start problem-solving is someone to help them dissolve the negative energy. You help them do this by listening in the following way:

1. You clear your mind of all thoughts about the situation, the person, the jobs you still have to do, etc.

2. You listen to get the person's experience. You want to get a real sense of what it is like to walk in his/her shoes at this moment.

3. You don't try to come up with any advice.

4. You reflect back to the person his feelings or thoughts with comments like, "Sounds like you're angry," or "sounds like you've been dealing with a lot of problems," or "I hear your concern about the deal falling through."

One of the two identical sets of circles below represents the thoughts and feelings of the person dealing with the situation. The other set represents your experience of the person's energy field.

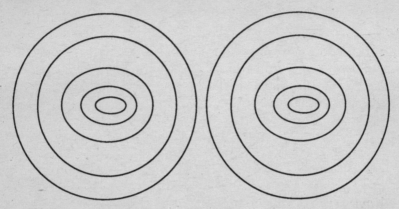

5. When you truly get a sense of how the other person is thinking and feeling (without judging, giving advice or trying to figure it out), the present form of the negative energy dissolves. When this happens, the person may forget what he or she is talking about, start laughing, or simply say, "I suddenly feel so much better." He or she now has more energy to use in achieving personal goals.

When to Use the Art of Dissolving

The art of dissolving is useful in the following situations:

1. When a customer is feeling negative about your product or service, allow the customer to talk as long as necessary while you use the process. Do not take any corrective measures until the negative energy is dissolved.
2. When a salesperson is feeling discouraged from dialing many numbers and not setting any appointments, dissolve the negative energy before giving additional training in telephone and appointment-setting skills.
3. If you are frightened that you won't reach your sales quota, express your fears with someone who can help you

dissolve them. Then focus on your tangible picture representing your sales quota.

4. When a family member is angry because you are spending so many hours on the job, allow the person to express his or her feelings without justifying the time spent at work. Then problem-solve to meet both people's needs.

It is important to use the art of dissolving with these and other situations before you problem-solve or provide skill-training. Otherwise, the negative energy acts as a block to creative thinking, learning, and producing.

CHECKING FOR UNDERSTANDING

Avoid Negative Programming

1. Your subconscious must create a way to produce the result you want that meets all the criteria you program into it.   T   F

2. You can absorb other people's feelings into your energy field just like a dry sponge absorbs water.   T   F

3. You can create results without consciously knowing you are doing so.   T   F

4. You are always conscious of what you're feeling.   T   F

5. You may program your subconscious from your right brain, and not know it.   T   F

6. Your subconscious accepts any thought and picture that's rehearsed enough times and coupled with feeling energy.   T   F

7. Your subconscious only produces goals that are linked to positive feelings.   T   F

8. Your subconscious has its own value system and conscience.   T   F

9. Things that seem like mistakes are   T   F
sometimes the results of your subconscious producing unconsciously created goals.

10. Your subconscious accepts your re-   T   F
peated description of what is true at the moment as the result you want produced.

Answers

1. T	6. T
2. T	7. F
3. T	8. F
4. F	9. T
5. T	10. T

IDENTIFYING UNCONSCIOUS PROGRAMMING

Information: The purpose of this activity is to help you identify how you are unconsciously programming your subconscious through the various media and the people with whom you spend your time. Once you see what information you are feeding into your subconscious through what you see, hear, and do, you can make conscious choices about the changes you want to make.

Directions: Use a separate sheet of paper to do the following activities:

1. Make a list of the television shows you watch and the dominant theme of each show such as "putting people down, answering trivia questions, educational, sensationalism, murder mystery, dog-eat-dog relationships, family shows, humor," etc.

2. Make a list of the music you hear repeatedly and the dominant themes such as, "lost love, life is hard, love is forever," etc.

3. Make a list of the people with whom you spend time and the dominant themes of your conversations with each person such as "the success you have had, the trouble someone is having, the high price of things, the condition of business or the government, how the fish are biting," etc. (Do this for people at work, home, school, places of recreation, etc.)

4. Make a list of the materials you read and the dominant theme of the materials such as humor, education, current events, etc. Identify whether the content of the materials is predominantly positive or negative. (Note: If something you read results in your feeling scared, sad, hopeless, or other unwanted feelings, that would be classified as negative reading material. If you read about a condition that is deplorable, and you feel outraged, determined to correct the situation, and confident that you *can* correct it . . . that would be classified as positive reading material. However, if it leaves you feeling helpless and powerless to do anything about it, it is negative reading material.)

POSITIVE AFFIRMATIONS

Directions: Repeat these affirmations on a daily basis to internalize the principles of your subconscious, and hasten the achievement of your desired results.

1. If I have a situation in my life that is not what I want, I don't continue to think about the way it is . . . I see it and tell it the way I want it to be.

2. I don't unconsciously create negative goals by worrying about things. Instead, I rehearse the positive achievement of my chosen goals.

3. I am careful to be conscious of what I am programming into my subconscious through television, radio, newspapers, and other media.

4. I pay conscious attention to the music I hear, and I listen

only to music that helps me create an abundance of good for me and others.

5. I don't absorb other people's negative energies. I maintain my own positive energy level.

6. I no longer hold on to negative experiences from the past. I learn what I can from them, let them go, and create positive experiences.

7. I talk positively about my product, my customers, my associates, and my business.

8. I easily dissolve negative energy for myself and others whenever needed.

Secret Six

*Realize the Power
of Your Self-Image*

PREVIEW OF SECRET SIX

REALIZE THE POWER OF YOUR SELF-IMAGE

In Secret Six, you will learn the principles governing your self-image. You learn how changing jobs and/or roles without updating the pictures you hold of yourself limits your productivity and income. You also find out that while it is possible to achieve beyond your self-image, it is not possible to maintain that achievement for any length of time without expanding your self-image.

This Secret also explains how an understanding of object relations theory helps solve problems such as having a string of no sales, giving up after your prospect says no the first time, buying into your prospect's negative views of your product, and fearing that your long-term deals will fall through.

REALIZE THE POWER OF YOUR SELF-IMAGE

WHAT IS THIS THING CALLED SELF-IMAGE?

Your self-image consists of the pictures you have of yourself in your imagination. These pictures are developed during your formative years, and unless you make a conscious effort to change them, they remain basically the same throughout your life. You have pictures of yourself as a manager, a salesperson, a closer, a prospector, a creative person, a healthy person, a husband/wife, a parent/uncle/aunt, son/daughter, etc. You can have a positive or negative feeling about each of the many roles you fulfill. As you unconsciously add up how you think and feel about yourself in each of these areas, you develop a predominantly positive or negative feeling about yourself in general.

You probably call this overall feeling about yourself your "self-image," thinking that you have only one self-image and it's basically either positive or negative. The truth is that you have as many pictures of yourself as you have roles you play, which adds up to many self-images.

While your attitudes and beliefs influence your reality, your self-image is the CEO of the company. It carries the most weight and runs the show. Your image determines which talents you will use, and in a sense, governs your potential.

If you get the desire to be the top salesperson in your company, that desire gets submitted to your subconscious. It checks to see

148

how your desire matches the picture you hold of yourself as a salesperson. If it matches, it is easy to become the top salesperson. If it doesn't match, your self-image says, "No, that isn't me. I just don't see myself like that. I see me more as an average achiever . . . more of a middle-of-the-road salesperson." Your self-image then limits you to functioning as an average achiever no matter how much fine sales training you receive.

In the pages that follow, you will learn more about the importance of self-images and how to expand your present ones to reach the goals you have set for yourself. You will also learn the basic principles of how your self-images function.

PRINCIPLES OF YOUR SELF-IMAGES

Principle Number One: What You See Is What You Are

Although you have thoughts and feelings about who you are and what you do, it is the pictures you form from these thoughts and feelings that carry the most weight.

Your subconscious takes these pictures formed in your imagination and works twenty-four hours a day to make them real in your life. That's why the way you see yourself is so important. What is happening in your life now is a result of the pictures you hold of yourself in your imagination (your self-images).

Principle Number Two: Reality Follows Self-Image

Reality always follows the picture you hold of yourself. Whenever you set a goal to achieve something you have not done before, you must first see yourself as you want to be, not as you are. This is confusing to some people, because they have a hard time seeing themselves as successful at a task when they are just beginning to learn the skills required to perform the task. It is sometimes difficult for beginning salespeople to see themselves as successful when they have made no sales or only a few sales.

It is equally difficult for some seasoned professionals to see themselves achieving to the level of the "superstars" of the company. It's as if their minds are saying, "After you achieve the result, I'll believe you can do it."

This isn't the way your subconscious works. It takes the image you have of yourself *today*, and works to make *today's* reality fit that picture. That is why it is important to see yourself as successful *now*, not in the future, for your reality follows your image.

If you are new in selling, and haven't made your first sale, chances are you are thinking, "I know I'm going to have some sales soon (next week, after I learn the presentation better, etc.)." If your thoughts are of sales in the future, your results will always be out there in the future, like the carrot that is always out in front of the horse. Instead, you must see yourself selling now.

Since reality follows image, your activities are determined by your pictures of yourself. For example, if you see yourself as a person who is always late, you will oversleep or plan too many things to do in a period of time, to fulfill that image of being late.

It is important then, to picture yourself now *as you* want *to be.*

If you have difficulty seeing yourself differently from the way you presently are, the tangible pictures you made in Secret Three will solve this problem. Looking at them while experiencing your feelings about the result causes your brain to reproduce that picture in your imagination. Remember, what you see is what you get!

Principle Number Three: Expand Your Self-Images to Expand Your Reality

If you want to do something you've never done before or achieve to a much higher level, you get training for the new achievement, or put forth extra effort to reach a higher level—only to find that you are not getting the hoped-for results. Learning the basic skills required for the achievement without first expanding your self-image, is like trying to put a roof on your house without first putting up the walls. Just as a roof needs support, your new achievements need an internal picture of you having achieved them, or they don't happen.

Perhaps you receive field-tested training for the new achievement, or put forth extra effort, and are momentarily successful. However, you soon find yourself gradually fizzling out or reverting to your previous level of accomplishment. This happens because you have only temporarily expanded your self image in addition to increasing your skill level. Unless this new, expanded self-image is reinforced until it is accepted by your subconscious, subsequent achievements don't happen, or present achievements are soon lost.

The first step in reaching a desired result is expanding your present self-image to include this achievement.

Principle Number Four: Success May Bring Up Hidden Beliefs

To expand your self-image, you must clear out any negative attitudes and beliefs about the goals you want to achieve. As you begin to achieve greater success, deep-seated beliefs about yourself and success may begin to surface. At times they may battle with your new desires and goals, causing you to experience tension and anxiety. You may think you have a fear of success or a fear of failure, when in reality it is simply the surfacing of old beliefs.

For example, if you've set a goal to double your income, but have a hidden negative belief about rich people, your production may be affected as you try to cope with the struggle between the new goal and your negative feelings. Often you will see-saw back and forth between increased sales and dry spells, as you try to reach your goal of increased income, while also trying to avoid becoming one of those "rich people." The answer to this dilemma lies in emptying your mind of negative beliefs about "rich people."

MORE SALES TRAINING ISN'T ALWAYS THE ANSWER

Some common problems experienced by salespeople and sales managers are as follows:

1. Person gets promoted because of consistently good performance, but then his/her performance gradually slips, and the position is lost.
2. The salesperson's closing average suddenly improves greatly, then just as suddenly reverts to its usual level, and stays there.
3. A lackadaisical salesperson with great potential produces a below-average amount despite much training.
4. A conscientious, responsible salesperson with unlimited income potential plods along, satisfied with mediocre income.
5. A salesperson is a superstar for years, then suddenly the bottom falls out.

Often the fine sales training provided by companies solves the problems mentioned above. However, there are times when more sales training isn't the answer, because the problem stems from self-image issues as you will see in the following examples.

This first example illustrates the problem of the salesperson who is promoted because of consistently good performance, but fails to live up to expectations and loses the position.

Example: You're Bad—You Never Will Amount to Anything

The idea that you're bad and will never amount to anything can come from your parents or other authority figures, or it can be a conclusion you made on your own as a child.

Sarah is an example of a person who drew this conclusion about herself early in life. She had an older brother and two older sisters who did very well in school. Pleasing the teacher was the highlight of their day. Although Sarah had above average intelligence, she didn't enjoy school, and seldom finished her assignments.

Because of this, she judged herself to be bad, and concluded that she'd never amount to anything because she didn't fit into the mold set by the school system as did her brother and sisters. She compared herself to them and didn't measure up. The image she held of herself as bad, (not fitting in at school) and never amounting to anything, (not doing well in school) was neatly stored away in her subconscious.

After finishing high school, Sarah found her niche in life. She took a job in a large department store, and after two years was promoted to assistant manager. Over a period of time, her performance began to slip. She didn't get records in on time. She did a poor job of scheduling her employees, and even started coming in late herself. After a number of warnings, Sarah was demoted to her old position.

Sarah worked hard and again was promoted to assistant manager. In this position, her performance once again slipped, and this time the store decided to let Sarah go. She soon found new employment, and after several years was again promoted to a position of responsibility. Fortunately, along with the promotion came management training. It was during the training workshop that Sarah discovered the phenomenon of "Now I've Got It, Now I Don't."

She became aware of the negative beliefs she had formed about herself, and changed them to positive ones. This resulted in a more positive self-image which increased her level of performance. This led to her being promoted to store manager by her new company, and this time she was able to successfully fulfill the role.

This second example illustrates the problem of the salesperson whose closing average suddenly improves and just as suddenly reverts to its previous level.

Example: Self-Image Impacts Closing Average

Sue worked as a secretary for fifteen years prior to entering sales. During the first ten years of work, her highest hourly wage was $12 per hour. Over the next five years, Sue received a number of promotions finally reaching the position of executive secretary earning $25 per hour.

Doubling your income per hour is a good achievement. For someone earning commissions of several hundred dollars or more in an hour, $25 an hour might seem small, but for Sue it was very exciting to be making that much money.

After working for three years as an executive secretary, Sue decided she wanted to be in sales. From the very beginning of her new career, her closing average was one out of every eight presentations, and stayed there for six months. Then she made a large number of sales in one week. This raised her closing average to one out of three presentations. She was elated. However, Sue made no more sales for the next few weeks. The number of presentations she made without sales during that time brought her closing average back to one out of eight.

When she totaled the figures for the seven months she had been selling, she found her average commission per sale came to $228. When she divided this by the eight presentations she had to give to make one sale, her average commission came to $28.50 per hour. Remember, prior to entering sales, Sue's highest income as a secretary had been $25 per hour.

Even though Sue had left her secretarial position, and had unlimited opportunity for income, her average hourly income actually stayed about the same. Why? The answer lies in Sue's self-image, and the way she viewed herself in regards to earning power. Sue's self-image as a salaried person with an income of $25 per hour prevented her from maintaining the higher closing average which she achieved for a short period of time. The higher closing average resulted in much more income per hour, which didn't fit her internalized self-image.

Sue had followed in the footsteps of her mother and grandmother who had both spent their adult lives as salaried secretaries. Sue identified so much with her family, that although she had changed jobs, she hadn't changed her internal image of herself. What Sue needed was training to help her become aware of her outdated expectation. She needed to begin seeing herself as a commissioned salesperson with no ceiling of hourly wages, rather than as a salaried secretary.

Sue's story has a happy ending. While attending a *Secrets of SuperSelling* workshop, she became aware of two things: first, she realized the limits she was placing on herself by accepting the family tradition of being tied to earning hourly wages, and second, the corresponding guilt she felt over making easy commissions. Along with following the other Secrets presented in the workshop, she updated her image through positive denials, affirmations, and visualizations, and went on to become one of the top salespeople in her company.

Here is the list of positive denials and affirmations that helped her change her old beliefs and expand her limiting self image.

1. It's not true that my family won't love me if I am different from them.
2. It's okay for me to earn more than my mother and grandmother earned.
3. I'm not stuck at $25 per hour. It's okay for me to make much more than that.
4. I am not a secretary any longer. I am a professional, commissioned salesperson, with no ceiling on what I earn.
5. Selling is not hard. Selling is easy, and I make much more money selling than I did as a secretary.

She was also instructed to create tangible pictures that illustrated the ideas covered in the preceding denials and affirmations.

Sales training is both valuable and necessary, but it must include methods to help you expand your self-image as you change careers and learn new skills. Otherwise, your old self-image limits your success.

This third example illustrates the problem of the salesperson whose production stays the same despite much sales training and potential.

Example: Don't Do Better Than Me

Rick is a car salesman. His boss was excited about his potential, and expected great things of him. However, these great expectations did not materialize. When Rick attended the *Secrets of SuperSelling* workshop, he was barely making ends meet. In one of the class experiences, he was asked, "What was your father's top income per year?" In Rick's case, it was just a few hundred dollars over what Rick was making selling cars.

What Rick Found Out

While many families tell you out loud to "Go get'em, Tiger," they also give a silent message that says, "But don't do better than us!" A country song sums it up as, "Don't Get Above Your Raisin'." It appeared that this message had stuck in Rick's subconscious. He didn't feel right making more money than his dad.

Through his work with one of the authors, Rick became aware of what was holding back his sales potential. Along with following the other Secrets, he began using the following positive denials and affirmations regarding his self image:

1. It's okay for me to earn more money than my dad ever earned.
2. My dad won't be jealous of me, because I am earning more than he did.
3. I am no longer barely making ends meet. I always have more money than I need.

Rick soon began meeting his income goals easily, and still maintained his close relationship with his father.

This fourth example illustrates the problem of people with unlimited income potential who earn mediocre incomes.

In today's complex job market, people find themselves in ever-changing situations. Due to increases in technology, their jobs may be eliminated, or in an effort to improve their lifestyle, they may change to a new profession entirely.

Promotions and job changes frequently bring along with them a change in roles. Unless you update your subconscious with new data based on the differences and similarities of your new position, you may limit yourself in one of the following ways:

1. You may find yourself treating the two positions as if they are the same.
2. You may scare yourself by seeing the two positions as totally different, thus decreasing your effectiveness.

Example: Social Worker/Realtor Sees Two Positions as the Same

Ann was a real estate agent who had functioned very effectively as a social worker for many years. After selling real estate for a period of time, she was dissatisfied with her level of income. Most of Ann's clients were people of limited means. It took a long time to find a house that would suit them in the price range they could afford. Their income level limited her sales to the $30,000 to $40,000 range.

While attending a *Secrets of SuperSelling* workshop Ann was asked to take a look at the similarities and differences between her two professions. As a social worker she used to help people get set up on food stamps, get medical care, and so on. Now she helped similar people get housing they could afford. She began to see that she was treating the two jobs as if they were the same. By doing this she was limiting her sales potential by defining her new position as "helping people find houses," rather than "selling real estate." She immediately set about updating her self-image with this new information. She began telling herself, "I'm not a social worker anymore, and I don't work with disadvantaged people. I'm no longer on a fixed salary with hours set by an agency. I'm a super real estate saleswoman. I sell homes easily and quickly to qualified buyers. I'm no longer on a fixed income."

Ann also set specific money goals.
Within one year, her average sale had risen
from $35,000 to $100,000.

Example: Salesman—Sales Manager . . . Person Sees the Two Positions as Different

Jim was a top-notch salesman who was promoted to sales manager. He found himself worried and tense. He felt ineffective in his new role because his salespeople weren't producing at the level he thought appropriate for their abilities. This disturbed him greatly since he had a strong need to "make the sale," and do a good job at whatever he did. He was thinking, "I know how to sell, but I don't know how to get *them* to sell!"

When Jim enrolled in the *Secrets of SuperSelling* workshop he was scared of his new job as sales manager. He had convinced himself that it was totally different from his successful role as salesman. After expressing these thoughts, he was asked to list the similarities and differences between the two roles. He came up with the following ideas:

Salesperson: As a salesperson, I convince the buyer of the value of my product or service. My income is dependent only on my personal production.

Sales Manager: As a sales manager, I convince salespeople of the value of the company's product, service, sales training, etc. I also convince them to use the company's sales techniques.

Before consciously comparing the two roles, Jim had gone around thinking, "Gosh, I used to sell insurance. Now I'm managing people. I don't know how to manage salespeople, but I sure can sell insurance." This produced some anxiety. As his subconscious got the message, "I don't know how to manage salespeople." He found himself saying and doing the wrong things with his staff. (Remember, your subconscious takes what you say literally, and will do whatever is necessary to carry out the order it receives. In Jim's case the order was, "Don't know how to manage salespeople.")

When Jim began looking at the similarities and differences in the two jobs, he was able to see that he could transfer the skills that he used so successfully as a salesman to his new job of managing his salespeople. He was still selling, it was just that his product had changed. This helped him to relax, increased his confidence level, and boosted his effectiveness with his staff.

With these new insights, Jim got busy visualizing his salespeople buying his ideas, just as his customers used to buy his product. He made tangible pictures of himself handing out production awards to his staff, just as they used to be awarded to him. In addition, he created pictures of himself receiving awards now for his group's production just as he used to get them for his individual sales. Within three months, his sales force had doubled production.

In the first example, Ann, was limiting her potential by seeing her new job as similar to her previous one. In the second example, Jim was having difficulty because he was concentrating too much on the job differences.

Through spaced repetition of positive denials and affirmations and the use of visualizations, you can update your self-image to fit your new role. Just getting a new job, a new briefcase and new clothes isn't enough. Along with changing the external factors, you must make the necessary internal changes in your subconscious.

This fifth example illustrates the problems faced when the bottom suddenly falls out for the superstar.

Example: Bittersweet Success

Bill had a short-term goal of doing the very best job he could each day. However, he did not consciously set a long-term goal of being a business owner and having a substantial net worth.

Many of the people Bill worked with were high achievers. Most of them had more income than he had, and owned nicer things than he did. However, because of his doing the very best he could each day, it wasn't long before he caught up with them. He acquired great possessions, a large income, and had a lovely family.

Just as Bill was riding high, his world began to collapse. Almost overnight he found himself involved in a divorce. His good credit rating slipped away. His net worth, which had been considerable, was lowered to almost nothing. He started spending time with people who had lower goals, and little or no money.

Later, while participating in a *Secrets of SuperSelling* workshop, Bill came to a number of realizations. The internal picture he held of himself did not include the income and net worth he had achieved. He did not see himself as the owner of a business. He had never set a conscious goal to be that financially successful. He wasn't doing his daily activities to become the owner of the business; he was just doing the best he could each day.

Bill had achieved beyond his internalized picture of himself. If he had realized what was happening, he could have simply enlarged his internal picture, so that it matched his abilities and accomplishments.

Expanding your self-image is the same as adding a room onto your house to accommodate your larger family. As you grow and develop more of your potential, you must change and modify the internal image you have of yourself. Along with striving for what you want, you must create an internal image of yourself that says, "Yes, that is me!"

As you move along through life, keep track of your internal

image just as you keep track of the condition of your car, home, or wardrobe. Check your image to see that it is in line with your talents, desires, and achievements. Update it as needed just as you do your car or wardrobe. Updating and expanding your self-image allows you to use and enjoy your talents and abilities more fully. It also allows you to keep the good things you get.

> ***The point of these stories is that it is just as necessary to set intangible goals to update your self-image as it is to learn basic selling skills.***

The other situations in which sales training isn't always the answer include:

1. Having a string of "no sales."
2. Feeling personally rejected when a prospect says no to your product or service.
3. Being told, "I'll buy this in two months when I've paid off current obligations." You worry whether or not the customer will follow through.
4. After several prospects "bad mouth" your product or service, you begin to feel the same way about it, and are soon selling something else.
5. A prospect objects, and you stop selling after the first few no's.

These are familiar situations for salespeople. For some, the stress involved in the situation causes the salesperson to slip back to an earlier level of development. This makes it temporarily impossible to use the fine sales skills he or she already possesses.

To understand the cause and to solve the problem, we need to examine Object Relations Theory which explains the developmental stages we all go through as we learn to relate to other people and things.

UNDERSTANDING OBJECT RELATIONS THEORY

At birth you were not aware of self and others. A short time later you became aware of yourself and mother, but experienced the two of you as one and the same.

The next step in your development was the awareness that you and your mother were separate people. However, you still experienced mother, other people, and things as one and the same. At that stage in your development, you were still unable to tell the difference between your mother, your father, your bottle, or blanket.

The next stage in your development was the discovery that mother, father, bottle, blanket, etc., were different. At this point, however, you had not yet reached the level of object constancy. This means that while you recognized the difference between objects, you were still not certain they existed unless you could see or hear them. If mom left the room, you probably started to cry. When she was out of sight, you were not sure she was still around, and probably stopped crying only when she reappeared.

Eventually, you reached the level of object constancy. You finally knew that mom and all other objects existed, even when you couldn't see or hear them.

Reaching the level of object constancy does not mean that you never again have trouble telling the difference between yourself and others. Under stress, even as an adult, you may experience the earlier stages of development. For example, if your friend has a craving to eat a sandwich, you may begin to feel the same craving. If you go on a number of job interviews and don't get the job, you may expect the next interviewer to act the same as the ones before. Both of these situations might be the result of your operating at an earlier level of development.

In the next section you will see how object relations theory helps explain problem situations experienced by salespeople and managers. You will also find suggested steps to help you increase your effectiveness in selling.

HOW OBJECT RELATIONS THEORY RELATES TO SELLING

In these first two examples, the salespeople are operating at the stage of development where a person can't tell the difference between self and others.

Salesperson Stops Selling After the First No

When the salesperson stops selling after the first one or two no's, it may be because he is caught up in the "story" of the customer. He sees himself and the customer as the same, just as the infant at one stage of development sees itself and others as the same. As the customer gives reasons for not buying the product or service, the salesperson agrees with the customer and "buys" into the objections, because he experiences himself and the customer as one and the same.

Example: If the customer says, "I can't afford it," the salesperson stops selling rather than helping the customer work out a sensible plan for fitting the desired item into the budget. Or, if the customer says, "I'll have to think about it," the salesperson stops selling rather than helping the customer make the decision to think and choose now.

Customers "Bad Mouth" the Product or Service

Another time when a salesperson may not be able to separate self and others is when a customer bad-mouths the product.

Example: Sam calls on several people who don't want his product or service. They bad-mouth the item he is marketing. Not being able to tell the difference between the customers and himself, he begins to take on the same feelings about the product or service as those who run it down. Soon he is selling something else.

Action Steps to Separate Self and Others:

1. Write these positive denials and affirmations and read them daily. "I am not under stress. I am calm and confident. I am a separate person at all times. I don't get caught up in other people's thoughts and feelings. I am able to think my own thoughts at all times. I am comfortable sharing my thoughts with others, even when they are different from theirs."

2. Practice handling objections with friends or colleagues. See if you can get them to go where you want to go if there is a difference in opinion as to choice of restaurant or show. Be careful to keep your feelings, beliefs, and desires separate from theirs.

3. Take every chance you get to have a conversation with someone who thinks differently from you. See if you can persuade them to change their mind on an issue. This helps you maintain your own line of thinking in the face of differing thoughts.

A String of No Sales

In this example, the salesperson is operating at the level of development where a person can't tell the difference between one person and another.

Example: Sarah goes on a sales call. The customer doesn't buy. Sarah goes on another call. That person doesn't buy either. On each of her next calls, Sarah, is sure the customers won't buy. She experiences a string of "no sales."

Sarah is functioning at the level of not being able to tell the difference between people. She unknowingly sees the current prospect as acting the same as previous prospects. She "expects" each prospect to say no, and they live up to her expectations. She comforts herself with the thought that "sales is a numbers game."

Expectations Limit Sales

Here is another example of a salesperson who can't tell the difference between one person and another, but with a little twist.

Example: Bob's customers usually buy merchandise in the low- to medium-price range. He approaches each new customer with these same expectations even though many could buy more expensive items. Consequently, he continues to sell only medium-priced items.

Action Step to Tell the Difference Between People:

1. Write and read daily: "Not all people are the same. I don't carry over any unfinished business from one sales call to the next. Each situation is separate. I do the very best job I can with each one. I see each person (customer) as the unique individual he or she is. I give every person the room to make the right choice for him or her. I always reach my sales goals easily."

Salesperson Feels Personally Rejected When Customer Doesn't Buy

In this example, the salespeople are operating at the level of development where a person has difficulty separating self from things.

Example: Bret goes on calls and gets extremely upset when people don't buy. When the customer says "no," he takes it personally. Instead of seeing the prospect as not wanting the product, Bret feels the prospect has rejected him as a person. After repeated "no's," Bret's self-esteem is lowered to the point where he feels badly, and doesn't enjoy his job anymore.

Salesperson Hates Prospecting by Phone

The following is another example where the salesperson is operating at the level of development where a person has difficulty separating self from things.

Example: Georgina owns an advertising service. She knows that one of the best prospecting tools in her trade is the telephone. However, she finds herself freezing up every time she starts to call a prospective customer. She often stops calling after receiving two or three "no's." She sees them as rejections of herself rather than the person not being interested in her service at this time.

Action Step to Separate Self and Things:

1. Write and read daily. "I am a worthwhile person whether or not people like or buy my product. Not liking my product doesn't mean people don't like me. I am completely separate from what I sell."

Now I Want It . . . Now I Don't

In this next example, the person is operating at the level of development where a person can't tell the difference between objects.

Example: Jennifer is a commissioned saleswoman. As long as she could remember, she had wanted an expensive ring. One day she found just the right one, but the store would not increase her credit line sufficiently to buy the ring that day. She decided to put some money down on it, and place the ring on lay-away.

After two weeks had passed, Jennifer found herself worn out from buying things and returning them. She bought both personal items and household goods, and eventually took each one back. This was unusual behavior for her. Being a salesperson, she was careful about what she bought and very seldom returned items she purchased.

She began to get concerned about her sales production since so much of her time was being consumed buying and returning items. Each day she found herself wanting to get the ring, and instead, going out and buying something she could afford . . . but didn't really want. Under stress, she was functioning at the level of not being able to tell the difference between things. She went to the store and bought something that her credit limit would allow. Getting something reduced her stress level. Then, she was able to see that she didn't really want the item. Back to the store she would go. Getting new clothing was not the same as getting the ring!

Finally, she realized what was happening, and set out to use the time she'd been spending buying and returning items to sell her product. This resulted in increased sales, which soon allowed her to pick up the ring.

Action Step to Tell the Difference Between Objects:

1. Write and read daily: "Not all objects are the same. When I want something I can't have right away, I know that getting a substitute is not the same as getting what I really want. By concentrating on the action steps needed to achieve my goal, I get it quickly and easily."

Don't Count Your Chickens Until They're Hatched

In this last example the salesperson is functioning at the level of not being sure something exists unless it can be seen, or is happening right then.

Example: Jerry goes on a sales call. The customer promises to buy two months from the time of the appointment. There is a firm, verbal commitment. There may even be a purchase order dated two months later.

As time goes on, Jerry becomes more and more anxious about whether or not this deal is going to go through. As the thought of, "I hope nothing messes this up," get coupled with feelings of doubt and fear, his subconscious gets the message that this deal is not supposed to close. It is to get messed up and somehow it does.

Action Step to Know Things Exist Even When Out of Sight:

1. Write and read daily: "It's not necessary for me to have the signed check in my hand to believe this deal is going through. I see the check in my hand on the day they have agreed to pay me. I am not worried. I am confident."

How Understanding Object Relations Theory Can Improve Your Self-Image

If you experience a string of no sales, a deal falling through that was supposed to close in a few weeks, or any of the other behaviors listed in this section, your self-image may be affected negatively. You may chastise yourself for not having used the sales skills you have been taught. When you understand that under stress you functioned at a level of development that made it impossible for you to act any differently, you stop berating yourself. You accept the fact that you are simply behaving the way many normal human beings behave under stress. You are excited that the situation can be easily changed through the action steps listed, and your self-image becomes more positive. You once again are in touch with your personal power, and reach your sales or management goals.

CHECKING FOR UNDERSTANDING

Realize the Power of Your Self-Image

1. If your sales skills are good, your self-image doesn't matter.   T   F
2. Wanting to be liked by your family may limit your sales.   T   F

3. The internal picture you have of yourself is more powerful than your thoughts and feelings.   T   F

4. It is possible to create results that are greater than the internal picture you have of yourself.   T   F

5. Your subconscious eventually makes reality match your self-image.   T   F

6. At birth you are unable to tell the difference between yourself and other objects.   T   F

7. Once you develop the ability to differentiate between yourself and others, you never lose it.   T   F

8. Under stress you may take on the negative feelings of the customer about your product.   T   F

9. Important people in your life can set unconscious ceilings on your accomplishments.   T   F

10. When you've achieved beyond your self-image, your self-image will usually catch up with your new level of achievement.   T   F

Answers

1. F	6. T
2. T	7. F
3. T	8. T
4. T	9. T
5. T	10. F

DISCOVERING YOUR SELF-IMAGE

Information: You have many self-images corresponding to the many different roles you play. The different self-images add up to either a predominantly positive or negative view of yourself.

By identifying your self-image about money, your business, relationships, sex, health, exercise, sports, and such, you can see what you need to add or dissolve to create the self-image you choose for yourself.

Directions: Take a sheet of paper and write at the top, "What I think and feel about _____ ." In the blank space write one item such as selling, prospecting, closing, money, my marriage, my weight, etc.

Write as quickly as possible all your thoughts and feelings about the subject mentioned. You may want to talk into a tape recorder and write it out later.

Example: What I Think And Feel About Exercise

"Exercise is hard. I look good when I go in, but I sweat while I work out. I have to shower before I leave. It is good for my body. It helps me avoid heart attacks. It is fun when I do it with other people. It has to be done three or four times a week to be effective. It is necessary for good muscle tone. If there is no pain, there is no gain. Exercise clubs are nice, but expensive. There's also the expense of exercise clothes."

Directions: Separate the negative ideas from the positive ones as in the example that follows:

Negative: "Exercise is hard. I look good when I go in, but I sweat while I work out. Then I have to shower before I leave. Clubs are expensive and I'd have to buy special clothing. I'd have to go three or four times a week and people say there is no gain without pain."

Positive: "Good for my body. Helps avoid heart attacks. Fun with other people. Necessary for good muscle tone. Clubs are nice."

Directions: Next, you write positive denials for any negative ideas you want to dissolve. Here you have a choice. You don't have to dissolve all the ideas that you consider negative. You can dissolve the idea that clubs are expensive and you must always look good, thereby allowing yourself to go to clubs, or you can choose to keep the ideas and exercise at home alone or with your friends.

Now, write out your ideal self-image using the positive ideas you already have. Add to this any other ideas needed to create your desired self-image.

Example: What I Think and Feel About Exercise

"Exercise is easy. I no longer believe there is no gain without pain. It is great fun to exercise with other people. I am happy when I'm exercising because I know it is helping me keep my heart in good shape. I'm increasing my muscle tone. I enthusiastically exercise three or four times a week. My exercise keeps my metabolism working so well that I am able to eat everything I want and still maintain my ideal body weight of _____ and fat ratio of _____ percent."

Directions: Repeat this process for your many roles, relationships, activities, and things such as:

- selling
- prospecting
- cold calling
- my company
- health
- being a mother
- being a father
- being the baby of the family
- my father
- my mother
- being the head of the company
- having to work my way up from the bottom
- money
- my checkbook
- my sister
- my brother
- religion
- the church
- the government
- cars

Now make pictures to represent your positive self-images. Somewhere on the page, include the description of your desired self-image. Look at the pictures daily until you feel comfortable with your expanded self-image.

EXPANDING YOUR SELF-IMAGE

Directions: The following steps will help you to expand your present self-image.

1. Consciously choose what you want to be, do, and have.
2. While you are busy setting and reaching tangible goals for income, net worth, possessions, promotions, and the like, be sure to also set intangible goals. These include the following:
   a. Increased patience
   b. Stronger faith
   c. Increased enthusiasm
   d. Greater persistence
   e. Greater determination
   f. Feeling that you deserve what you want and are capable of achieving
   g. Feeling that you are of value to yourself and others
   h. Being comfortable with yourself even though you are different from your immediate family (or others)
   i. Being comfortable with having more fun, friends, talent, money, etc. than your relatives

(This is not the entire list. It's just a sample to stimulate your own thinking.)

3. Choose a person as a role model who has achieved to a level to which you aspire. Get a picture of this person and put it on a piece of paper. Write a statement that tells it the way you want it to be. Example: "I am just as happy (wealthy, healthy, enthusiastic, successful, etc.) as _____ ." (Write the name of your role model in the blank.) Having a picture of a real person who has done what you want to do, helps you believe you can do it too. You know it is "doable," because you know a real person who has done it. If you want to break a record in your

171

particular occupation or company, get a picture of someone who has broken a record. Affirm, "I set a new record in _____ just as _____ did."

4. Look at this picture frequently.
5. Follow additional steps found in Secret Four for consciously creating your magnetic energy field for this goal.

POSITIVE AFFIRMATIONS

Directions: Repeat these affirmations on a daily basis to internalize the principles of your subconscious, and hasten the achievement of your desired results.

1. I never lose anything I achieve, because the first thing I do is create a self-image that supports the achievement.
2. I have positive self-images that support all my goals.
3. I am continually expanding my self-images.
4. It is easy for me to see myself successfully achieving my goals.
5. I'm confident that I can and do successfully handle all situations.
6. I don't carry over unfinished business from one experience to another. Each situation that I encounter is separate. I do the best I can in each one and see each person as the unique individual he or she is.
7. I am a worthwhile person whether or not people like or buy my product. Not liking my product doesn't mean people don't like me. I am completely separate from what I sell.
8. Not all objects are the same. When I want something I can't have right away, I know that getting a substitute is not the same as getting what I really want. By concentrating on the action steps needed to achieve my goal, I get it quickly and easily.

THE
SECRETS
OF
SUPERSELLING

Secret Seven

What You Give Out Comes Back to You Multiplied

PREVIEW OF SECRET SEVEN

WHAT YOU GIVE OUT COMES BACK TO YOU MULTIPLIED

In Secret Seven, you learn the benefits of *Going The Extra Mile*, as described by Napoleon Hill. You read of wealthy men who understood the law of increasing returns and knew that What You Give Out Comes Back To You Multiplied. You learn how enthusiasm about your product or service can increase the number of referrals and repeat business from satisfied customers.

WHAT YOU GIVE OUT COMES BACK TO YOU MULTIPLIED

GOING THE EXTRA MILE

Napoleon Hill spent most of his life studying the great achievers of the world to determine what made them successful. One of their habits that he wrote about at great length was that of going the extra mile.

Going the extra mile means giving more and better service than that for which you are paid, and giving it with a positive mental attitude.

Benefits of Going the Extra Mile

Here are just a few of the many benefits you receive when you give more than is expected of you.

1. You have a greater chance of keeping your job if employment is scarce. When employment is high, you are able to command the best positions.
2. You receive favorable attention from those who can and will provide opportunities for you to advance yourself.
3. You become indispensable to the people you serve, which helps you receive more than average compensation for the service you provide.
4. You feel worthy of asking for more money. If you are only giving the amount of service for which you are paid, then obviously you are receiving all the pay you deserve.

5. You feel good about yourself which enhances your self-image.
6. Your imagination is increased, because you are inspired to continuously seek new and better ways of giving service.

Carnegie Develops Industrial Leaders

Andrew Carnegie developed more successful leaders of industry than any other great American industrialist. Most of them came up from the ranks of ordinary day laborers, and many of them accumulated much larger personal fortunes than they could have acquired without Mr. Carnegie's guidance.

The first test that Mr. Carnegie applied to any worker whom he desired to promote was determining to what extent the worker was willing to go the extra mile.

An example of this is the story of Charles M. Schwab. Mr. Carnegie discovered that Mr. Schwab, a day laborer in one of the steel plants, always performed more and better service than he was paid for. In addition, he did it with a pleasing mental attitude which made him popular among his fellow workers. He was promoted from one job to another until eventually, in 1901, he was made president of the United States Steel Corporation at a salary of $75,000 a year.

On some occasions Mr. Carnegie not only paid Mr. Schwab's salary, but gave him as much as $1,000,000 as a bonus. When Mr. Carnegie was asked why he gave Mr. Schwab a bonus larger than his salary, he replied, "I gave him his salary for the work he actually performed. I gave him the bonus for his willingness to go the extra mile, thus setting a fine example for his fellow workers."

Hardly anyone is compelled to go the extra mile, and seldom does anyone ever request that you give more service than that for which you are paid. Therefore, it must be done on your own initiative. The compensation comes in many different forms. Increased pay is a certainty. Promotions are inevitable. Favorable working conditions and pleasant relationships are sure. All these lead to economic security.

New Position Received From Going the Extra Mile

Many years ago an elderly lady was strolling through a Pittsburg department store, obviously killing time. She passed counter after counter without anyone paying attention to her. Since the clerks had spotted her as an idle "looker" who had no intention of buying, they made it a point of looking in the other direction when she stopped at their counters.

Finally the lady came to a counter where a young clerk smiled warmly and asked if he might be of some help to her. "No," she replied, "I am just waiting for the rain to stop so I can go home." "Very well, Ma'am," the young man replied, "may I bring you a chair?" Without waiting for her answer, he brought her a chair. After the rain stopped, the young man took the lady by the arm, walked her to the street and said good-bye. As she left she asked him for his card.

Several months later the owner of the store received a letter, asking that this young man be sent to Scotland to take an order for the furnishings of a home. The owner of the store wrote back that he was sorry, but the young man did not work in the home furnishings department. However, he explained that he would be glad to send an "experienced man" to do the job.

Back came a reply from Andrew Carnegie that no one would do except this particular young man. The elderly lady whom the young man had helped was Mr. Carnegie's mother, and the "house" he wanted furnished was Skibo Castle in Scotland. When the young man reached Scotland, he received an order for several hundred thousand dollars worth of household furnishings. He later became half-owner of the store; he was paid handsomely for going the extra mile.

The Opportunity to Earn What He Was Worth

Late one afternoon, William C. Durant, the founder of General Motors, walked into his bank after banking hours, and was granted a favor which should have been handled during banking hours. The man who granted the favor was Carol Downes, manager of the bank. He not only served Mr. Durant with efficiency, but he went the extra mile and added courtesy to the service. He made Mr. Durant feel that it was a real pleasure to serve him. The incident seemed trivial, and of itself was of little importance. Unknown to Mr. Downes, this courtesy was destined to have repercussions of a far-reaching nature.

The next day Mr. Durant asked Downes to come to his office where he offered him a position in his business. Downes accepted, and was given a desk in a general office where nearly a hundred other people worked. He was given a modest salary, and notified that the office hours were from 8:30 A.M. to 5:30 P.M.

At the end of the first day, when the bell rang announcing quitting time, Downes noticed that everyone rushed for the door. He sat still, waiting for the others to leave the office. After they had gone, he remained at his desk, wondering why everyone was in such a hurry.

Fifteen minutes later, Mr. Durant opened the door of his private office, saw Downes still at his desk, and asked if he understood that he was allowed to stop work at 5:30. "Oh, yes," Downes replied, "but I did not wish to be run over in the rush." Then he asked if he could be of any service to Mr. Durant. He was told he might find a pencil for the motor magnate. He got the pencil, ran it through the pencil sharpener and took it to Mr. Durant who thanked him and said "good night." From then on, Downes always remained at his desk after closing time until he saw Mr. Durant leave for the day. He was not paid to do so, and no one promised him anything for remaining.

Several months later Downes was called into Mr. Durant's office and informed that he had been chosen to go out to a new plant that had been purchased recently. His job was to supervise the installation of the plant machinery. Imagine that—a newcomer to the car industry being given an assignment of this magnitude in only a few months.

Without quibbling, Downes accepted the assignment and went on his way. Three months later, the job was completed and done so well, that Mr. Durant called Downes into his office to find out where he had learned so much about machinery. "Oh," Downes explained, "I never learned, Mr. Durant. I just found men who knew how to get the job done, put them to work, and they did it." As Downes turned to go, Mr. Durant said, "I forgot to tell you that you are the new manager of the plant you have installed, and your salary is $50,000 a year to start with."

The following ten years of association with Mr. Durant were worth approximately eleven million dollars to Carol Downes. He became an intimate advisor of the motor king, and made himself rich as a result.

It is likely that many of Downes' fellow workers envied him because they believed he had been favored by Mr. Durant because of pull or luck. Well, Downes did have an inside "pull" with Mr. Durant. He created that "pull" on his own initiative by going the extra mile.

He created it by remaining at his desk with the hope that he might be of service to his employer after the "rush" was over at 5:30 each evening. In addition, he created it by finding men who understood how to install machinery instead of asking Durant where or how to find such men. His story consists of a series of little tasks well-performed, in the right mental attitude.

Andrew Carnegie lifted no fewer than forty such men from the position of day laborers to millionaires. He understood the value of men who were willing to go the extra mile. Whenever he found such a man, he brought him into the inner circle of his business, and gave him an opportunity to earn "all he was worth."

People do things or keep from doing them because of a motive. The soundest of motives for the habit of going the extra mile is the fact that it brings many benefits to all who practice the habit.

THE LAW OF INCREASING RETURNS

The law of increasing returns explains why going the extra mile works. While energy is flowing from you, it increases in quantity, and either magnetizes your pictures, thoughts, and feelings to you, or repels anything different from them away from you. Let's look at examples of the law of increasing returns.

Example: You can give your energy out in an intangible way in the form of feelings. This happens when you get excited at a ball game. As people around you feel your energy, they get even more excited. This spurs you on to greater enthusiasm, and you find yourself among a charged-up group of fans having a good time.

As a manager of people, you can create enthusiastic energy for your company, your product, or your sales contest. As you radiate this energy out to your staff, they get excited about your goals just as the crowd gets excited about the game.

The same thing holds true in selling. Your feelings about your product or service are relayed to your customer by your energy. As you feel excited or proud of what you are selling, this feeling gets conveyed to your customer. Since the laws of energy dictate that what goes out comes back multiplied, your enthusiasm about your product or service increases as you talk. Just as excitement is contagious at a football game, excitement about what you're selling is contagious. Seeing this through your eyes, the customer appreciates the value in your product or service, and buys. Your energy is multiplied when they begin selling their friends on your product or service just as you sold them. Your business switches more and more from cold-calling, active prospecting, and advertising to handling referrals from satisfied customers.

A more concrete example of the law of increasing returns is the giving of bonuses to employees or quality service to customers. Quite often the person receiving your energy in the form of a bonus returns that energy to you multiplied in the form of greater devotion to duty and increased performance. The customers receiving your energy in the form of quality service return it to you in the form of increased loyalty and the referral of your product or service to others.

Wealthy Men Understand the Law of Increasing Returns

As a young boy, John D. Rockfeller had a salary of $3.50 a week and gave $1.80 of it to church and charity. As an adult, he gave everyone he met a brand new dime. He also tithed 10 percent from his total earnings. In 1855 he gave $9.50 in tithes. The next year his tithes were up to $28.37. By 1884 his tithe was $5,489.62.

His income then remained stationary for about ten years. By 1887, his tithes exceeded a quarter of a million dollars, and in 1890 they topped the million dollar mark. Between 1855 and 1934, he gave away $531 million dollars.

Andrew Carnegie made a fortune in steel and through giving away money. He started with nothing, and received more than $350 million in his lifetime. He gave money away knowing it was returning to him multiplied.

Andrew Mellon was a self-made millionaire who practiced giving large sums of money away secretly. He did it without others knowing, because he didn't want any negative thoughts getting into his mind and creating doubt about it returning to him multiplied. At Christmas he took outstanding bills owed him and burned them.

Meyer Guggenheim came to America almost flat broke. He believed that to be happy through money, he had to make other people happy too. He really believed that each time he gave away a dollar, he would get ten dollars or more back.

If you decide to try this, it is important that you give away only the amount of money that you can give freely and feel good about. It makes no difference whether that amount is twenty-five cents, one dollar, or thousands of dollars. The point here is that you must be able to give the money joyfully to a person or group and be willing to receive back many times more than you give.

WHAT YOU GIVE IS WHAT YOU GET

Although we have been talking about money, the law of increasing returns applies to other things as well as money. If you give your time freely to people who need help, others will give their time freely to you when you need help.

If you give possessions of yours away when you no longer have use for them, others will give things to you when they no longer have use for them. Give to others what you want for yourself. If you want money, give money. If you want referred leads, give others referred leads. If you want people to be friendly to you, be friendly to others. Whatever you give out to others returns to you multiplied.

I HAD NO IDEA I'D DO THIS WELL

The law of increasing returns is also seen in the cases of people accomplishing results far greater than they had anticipated when they originally set their goals. Stories are heard over and over of people who state they had no conscious thoughts of achieving to such a high level. They say things like, "I just started out to get a small part in a movie, and found myself receiving an Oscar," or, "I only started out to sell a group of people in one office, and suddenly found myself selling a company who has offices nationally."

MAKING TIME TO GO THE EXTRA MILE

Sometimes people believe they cannot go the extra mile and give special, personal service because of the time it would take to do so. If you work from a purely left-brain approach to goal achievement, this might hold true. Your left brain says things like, "There aren't enough hours in the day to do everything I need to do just to make my sales quota or manage my staff. In addition, I have all my personal duties, such as taking care of the family, the house, myself, plus banking, personal grooming, and saving some time for fun and relaxation. The last thing I need to do is something extra!"

The left brain uses the same reasons for not being able to listen to self-improvement tapes, or not having enough time to create a magnetic energy field to make goal-achievement easier. As you repeat the ideas related to "not having enough time," your subconscious accepts the ideas as goals to achieve, and you experience these results in your life.

To support the idea that you can give extra service, achieve high-level goals, and still have time for a personal life, we invite you to interview high achievers of your choosing. Find out how much they are doing, and how they organize their time and duties to accomplish all that they do.

One public figure who demonstrates high achievement is Pastor Paul Cho, head of the largest Christian church in the world. He handles the normal duties of a pastorate, such as preaching several sermons each Sunday, as well as organizing a world-wide church. In addition, he invests a minimum of three hours a day in prayer and meditation when things are going well. If there is a problem, he devotes five hours of his day to prayer and meditation.

All who have achieved permanent success have followed the practice of doing more than they were paid for doing. One of the most important dividends from going the extra mile is a changed mental attitude. This gives you more influence with people, more self-reliance, greater initiative, more enthusiasm, more vision and definiteness of purpose. These qualities of successful achievement bring you many benefits, for What You Give Out Comes Back To You Multiplied.

CHECKING FOR UNDERSTANDING

What You Give Out Comes Back to You Multiplied

1. Napoleon Hill found that a important   T   F
   trait of successful people was their
   willingness to go the extra mile.
2. Going the extra mile means giving more   T   F
   and better service than what is expected
   of you or that for which you are paid.
3. It is often foolish or a waste of time and   T   F
   effort to give more than is expected of
   you.
4. One of the advantages of going the extra   T   F
   mile is that you feel good about yourself
   which enhances your self-image.

5. Another advantage of giving more than is asked is that you become indispensable to the people you serve.　　T　　F

6. The law of increasing returns states that what you give out comes back to you multiplied.　　T　　F

7. The law of increasing returns explains why going the extra mile works.　　T　　F

8. It is impossible to relay your feelings about your product or service to your customer through your energy.　　T　　F

9. People who go the extra mile find they have a changed mental attitude.　　T　　F

10. It is important to make time to go the extra mile.　　T　　F

Answers

1. T	6. T
2. T	7. T
3. F	8. F
4. T	9. T
5. T	10. T

GOING THE EXTRA MILE

Directions: On a separate sheet of paper, list times when you have gone the extra mile in the past. In addition, list the results of your efforts. If you did not get the benefits described in this Secret, the cause could be one of the following:

1. You didn't believe anyone would notice that you had gone the extra mile.

2. You didn't believe the people involved would give you increased pay, etc.

3. Your self-image wasn't expanded yet to the point where you could accept that increased pay, etc.

To insure receiving the most benefits possible as a result of going the extra mile, use positive denials and affirmations to clear any limiting energy from your subconscious.

Examples:

- "I no longer believe that no one notices my extra effort. What I do is seen, appreciated, and well-compensated."
- "It's not true that gong the extra mile doesn't work. The principle works for me just as described."
- "I no longer believe that people won't be as good to me as I am to them. They are even better to me than I am to them."
- "It's not true that I don't deserve more money for what I do. I deserve $ _____ or more because I do an excellent job."

Directions: To discover how you can currently go the extra mile in your job or business, answer the following questions on a separate sheet of paper.

1. Where can you give more time?
2. Where can you give more personal attention?
3. Where can you give creative ideas?
4. If you were a customer of your business, what special attention would be meaningful to you?
5. How can you show your customers that they are more than a "number" or an "invoice?"

Once you have identified ways you can go the extra mile, make a habit of doing them on a regular basis. Keep track of how what you do in going the extra mile comes back to you multiplied.

POSITIVE AFFIRMATIONS

Directions: Repeat these affirmations on a daily basis to internalize the principles of your subconscious and hasten the achievement of your desired results.

1. I believe that my time is valuable and I deserve to be paid well.

2. I'm thrilled that what I give out to others comes back to me multiplied.
3. I don't compete—I cooperate and create.
4. I do everything joyfully and enthusiastically.
5. I do what I love, love what I do, and always expect the best.
6. I confidently give myself reasons why I can succeed in everything that I do.
7. I find creative ways to give extra service and still have plenty of free time.
8. I love to see and hear of other people's successes.
9. I believe that everything I need is available in abundance for me.
10. I trust my ability to create sales, money, love, fun, health, food, etc. in abundance.
11. I love myself and others unconditionally.
12. I'm proud that I always do my best.

THE
SECRETS
OF
SUPERSELLING

Secret Eight

Celebrate Your Successes

Preview of Secret Eight
Motivating With Rewards
Motivating With Celebrations
Discovering Celebrations That Spur You On
Deciding Which Events to Celebrate
Keeping Track of Your Successes
Celebrating Through Recognition
Checking for Understanding
Deciding on the Guidelines For Your Celebrations
Deciding What Celebrations Spur You On
Positive Affirmations

PREVIEW OF SECRET EIGHT

CELEBRATE YOUR SUCCESSES

In Secret Eight, you will discover the reasons for celebrating your successes not only at the completion of your goal, but also periodically along the way. You will learn the importance of choosing celebrations that are appropriate and personally meaningful. In addition to celebrations being fun, you will learn that celebrating actually increases the power of your magnetic energy field.

CELEBRATE YOUR SUCCESSES

MOTIVATING WITH REWARDS

In sales, rewards in the form of trips, plaques, and bonuses are often given for high achievement. These rewards act as incentives to spur salespeople on to reach their company's quotas or goals. Rewards usually have the following characteristics:

1. They are planned and announced ahead.
2. They are based on some kind of competition.
3. They are based on predetermined quotas.
4. They are given at the *end* of a contest or promotion period.
5. They are awarded to only a small percentage of the sales force.

When we look at the definition of reward, we see that it is something given or received for worthy behavior. The idea of rewarding worthy behavior is closely linked to the idea of punishing unworthy behavior. Therefore, if you feel you deserve a reward for reaching your goals, you may also feel you deserve a punishment for failing to reach them. While receiving rewards is fun, punishments are not. We are not saying that rewards are bad or should be eliminated. They work very effectively to spur some salespeople on to higher production. However, for others they provide blocks to achievement.

MOTIVATING WITH CELEBRATIONS

The dictionary defines celebration as the observation of an occasion with appropriate ceremony, festivity, or merrymaking. Celebrations have the following characteristics:

1. They can be spontaneous or planned ahead.
2. They promote affiliation and cooperation.
3. They can be as frequent as you like and at any point in time.
4. They can include everyone on the sales force.

In addition to motivation, celebrations inspire good results in goal achievement in general and sales in particular. As you examine the definition, you discover that there are things you can do to celebrate that do not fall into the category of "rewards." The following example shows the festive, merrymaking side of celebrations.

Example: Dan was a sales manager whose group had just become number one in their region in total production. He excitedly called home to share the news with his wife. The two of them decided it was time for a celebration. When Dan walked into the house, he was surprised to find crêpe paper strung around the living room along with signs that said, "Super Salesperson!" "When You're Hot, You're Hot!" "Do It Again!" His wife hugged and kissed him, then grabbed his hands and the two of them danced around the room happily shouting about Dan's and his group's success. They decided to continue the celebration by going out for the evening. This was truly a time of festivity and merrymaking. (If Dan had been single, he might have shared the news with a friend, and the two of them could have celebrated. He could have also decided to celebrate by himself.)

Celebrating can also take the form of a ceremony as illustrated in the following example.

Example: Sam is a salesman who always keeps a box of "bodacious" cigars on his desk. He celebrates each sale by smoking one of these cigars. When he started celebrating in this way, he was selling less than $10,000 a month. Eventually, he increased his sales to more than $300,000 a year, and he did this three years in a row. He attributes his success, in part, to his satisfying method of celebrating with the ceremony of smoking the cigar.

The preceding stories show that celebrations can be spur of the moment, or planned and regular. They can take an hour, an evening or the length of time it takes to smoke a cigar. You will discover that the variation of celebrations is almost endless. What is important is that you take time to celebrate your successes, and that you choose a way that has special meaning for you.

DISCOVERING CELEBRATIONS THAT SPUR YOU ON

While most sales rewards are planned for you by your company or your boss, celebrating your successes is usually your own responsibility. The key to success with celebrating is to experience things that really please you. In order to find the celebrations that truly satisfy, it is helpful to interview your three ego states to learn what they value. (For a more thorough explanation of transactional analysis and ego states, see Secret Nine.)

As we stated earlier in Secret Four, transactional analysis states that within each of us are three ego states: the Parent, Adult, and Child. They all have different interests and needs. Your Child ego state is curious, determined, funny, spontaneous, and creative. It controls 45 percent of your energy, and responds to life very much like little children do. Young children love surprises, and parties, and like to be recognized for having done well. Acknowledging and celebrating with the Child within you is a powerful way to insure continued success.

In addition to your Child ego state, you also have an Adult ego state that uses logic, deals with facts and figures, and processes what is going on right here and now. Your Adult enjoys going over all the intricacies of how you made the sale or reached your goal:

- how you found the prospects.
- how you gave the presentation.
- how you dealt with the objections.
- how you found just the right item for the customer, etc.
- how you solved a problem.

Finding someone who really listens as you tell how well you handled all the details of a sale or transaction is a powerful way to please your adult, and celebrate your successes.

Your Parent is the ego state that sets limits based on your values and beliefs. It nurtures you and others. When you are complimented by others for being responsible, dependable, and conscientious, your Parent swells with pride just as real parents beam when their children are recognized for an achievement. Hearing others acknowledge these qualities in you is a celebration for your Parent.

Another way you can celebrate is by having mental conversations between your Parent and Child ego states. For example, have your Child thank your Parent for setting appropriate limits such as not letting you stay in bed until noon on a day when you need to be at work early. Have your Child thank your Parent for being willing to let you achieve such a high level. Transactional analysis tells us that your Child cannot do anything unless your Parent says it is okay. Even though your Child controls 45 percent of your energy, it needs the permission of the Parent within you to focus its energy in a certain direction. Acknowledging yourself for what you have achieved is a celebration that gives you permission to continue achieving.

Interviewing your ego states is an on-going process, because your needs change from day to day. Rest assured that the time you invest in discovering what kind of celebrations will feel good to you will bring you many dividends.

As you think of ways to celebrate, do not judge the value of the celebrations by how much they cost. You may enjoy celebrating by buying yourself a paperback that costs only a few dollars just as much as you enjoy celebrating by purchasing yourself a new piece of clothing costing considerably more.

You may also want to give yourself non-monetary, short-term celebrations like the freedom to spend an hour, (the morning, or the whole day) doing whatever you want from moment to moment. This means you could take a leisurely bath, watch TV, read, jog, eat, sleep, go shopping, play golf, etc. You do each activity only as long as you want to, and you'll be amazed at how rejuvenating it is to have a block of time where you have no deadlines.

DECIDING WHICH EVENTS TO CELEBRATE

As well as deciding *when* and *how* to celebrate, you must also decide *which achievements* to celebrate. If you celebrate only when you make a sale or reach a major goal, you cut off a prime source of motivation. It is important to celebrate each of the necessary steps you take along the path to making the sale or achieving your overall goal. The little Child inside you wants recognition and fun as often as possible, not just once in a while when you do something really noteworthy.

For example, if your goal is to make twelve sales by the end of the month, you may want to celebrate at these key points:

1. After successfully using a new method of prospecting.
2. After setting a certain number of appointments.
3. After making the number of sales presentations you set for the week.
4. After successfully using a new closing technique.
5. After closing each sale.

The important point is that you enjoy celebrating as often as possible, for this spurs you on toward achieving greater and greater success.

Celebrating your success is a worthwhile activity if for no other reason than that it is fun to do. However, the main reason for celebrating your successes along the way to your major goals is that it increases the power of your magnetic energy field. As you learned in Secret Four, your energy field connects you with the people and situations needed for the achievement of your goals. The more powerful your energy field is, the quicker and easier you achieve your goals.

The process of celebrating, especially the excitement of physically jumping up and down, clapping your hands, shouting, or whatever else brings you joy and pleasure, increases your level of physical energy. This in turn increases the intensity of your feelings. As you learned in Secret One, feelings are a necessary factor in programming your subconscious. The greater the intensity of your feelings, the easier it is for your subconscious to produce your result.

As you celebrate by talking about having gotten one more appointment, or about successfully using a new closing technique, your voice is propelling your increased level of energy away from you. Your energy field is then drawing to you what you are talking about which is one more sale, or one more prospect, or a situation where you are successfully using a new closing technique.

The more you celebrate your successes, the more successful you become. As you increase the power of your magnetic energy field in this way, you find yourself easily surpassing your original target.

You may feel comfortable expressing your feelings by celebrating in a very enthusiastic way. On the other hand, you may be a quiet, reserved person who is not comfortable showing your excitement around others. If you are the latter, you are invited to try letting your excitement out in the privacy of your own office or home. Try celebrating enthusiastically about your successes for a period of time. Keep track of your production, and see for yourself the value of celebrating your successes with gusto.

KEEPING TRACK OF YOUR SUCCESSES

Recording your successes is a great way to inspire yourself on the days when some doubt creeps into your mind about your ability to sell or reach certain goals. As you review your past successes, you once again experience how you felt when you achieved those goals. You recall the action steps you took in order to reach that target. You find yourself thinking, "I will reach this new goal just as easily as I reached all those others."

On a daily or weekly basis, record your successes in a notebook. If your achievements are written up in the newspaper or in your company's newsletter, put those articles in your notebook. As you achieve the goals in your picture book, transfer those pictures into a special section of your notebook titled, "Goals Achieved." Be sure to review it briefly on a regular basis. Recording your successes and reviewing them regularly adds energy and power to your magnetic energy field.

Acknowledgment and Recognition Leads to Celebration

The information about celebrating your successes applies to business owners, sales managers or management at any level as well as it does to individual salespeople. When you are responsible for supervising others, you can increase their production by including celebrations as well as planning rewards.

Rewards work very well for some people. The idea of winning spurs them on to higher production without producing the fear of punishment for failure. However, there are some salespeople who shy away from competition, and do not buy into sales promotions or rewards based on reaching some predetermined goal. Even when everyone in the company can win a trip or get a bonus by meeting a certain quota, these people become immobilized by the fear that they won't make it. For them, celebrations work like a charm.

CELEBRATING THROUGH RECOGNITION

Celebrating through recognition works well with all salespeople, but especially with those who don't respond well to competition and planned rewards. As was mentioned earlier, rewards are usually given for making certain sales quotas. Many salespeople need more reinforcement and encouragement along the way to major goals than are offered by rewards.

Celebrating through recognition works well for these salespeople because the celebrations can take place frequently. This helps create the magnetic energy field that insures the successful achievement of the goals.

The first step in using celebrations with others is to vary the type of recognition you use to suit each individual's needs. Some salespeople respond best to verbal forms of recognition, and others to monetary recognition.

Verbal forms of recognition can be directed by you to the salesperson from any of your three ego states. Statements to your salespeople from your Parent might be:

"I'm very proud of the number of sales you have made this week."

"We're lucky to have you as part of our sales force."

"I appreciate the extra time and effort you have put into this promotion."

"Thank you for being so prompt with the report."

Sometimes your people will want to hear statements from your Child such as:

"I'm really excited about the number of sales you have made."

"When you're hot, you're hot. Go get'em, tiger!"

"We're beating the socks off _____ district!"

"Tell them to watch our smoke."

There are times when acknowledgment from your adult works wonders. Statements to your salesperson from your adult might be:

"I liked your step-by-step presentation, it was clear and concise."

"I'm impressed with the speed with which you have learned the sales presentation."

"I'm impressed by your realizing ahead of time what paperwork you will need from your prospect. Asking him to have that available for your first appointment is very efficient of you."

"Your strategy for increasing your sales is brilliant!"

Be sure to give your full attention to your salesperson when celebrating verbally. The most important recognition a person strives for is what Transactional Analysis calls "Time And Presence Stroking." Briefly stated, it means, have your mind where your body is when you are with a person. Focus all your attention on the person at that moment. Share as much of your energy as you can. You are not just complimenting that person, you are helping him or her create a magnetic energy field that is effortlessly drawing to the person what you are acknowledging. The time you are investing in this manner results in increased production.

In addition to celebrating through verbal recognition, some salespeople respond well to physical recognition. You might do this by shaking their hands, patting them on their backs, or putting your arm around their shoulders. Physical recognition when linked with verbal recognition is a strong form of motivation.

Writing your salespeople congratulatory letters, putting notes on their desks, or displaying their pictures in a prominent place with the details of their accomplishments written underneath them, are forms of acknowledgment that lead to celebration. As they read your letters over and over or share them with friends, their feelings of excitement and pride grow.

Almost everyone enjoys money, which is why most sales rewards are in the form of bonuses, trips, or prizes. Celebrations can also include money. What's nicer than a salesperson finding an envelope on his or her desk with a congratulatory note and a surprise bonus, or tickets for a trip. The difference between monetary rewards and monetary celebrations is the element of spontaneity and surprise. Instead of giving the salesperson a large bonus for reaching some preplanned sales quota, you might try giving smaller surprise bonuses for a number of smaller accomplishments. This takes care of the Child ego state that often loses interest in striving for long-term rewards, but is spurred on by more frequent recognition. (If you acknowledge smaller accomplishments in this way, be sure to acknowledge the same accomplishments for each salesperson.)

A final point on celebrating through recognition. Be sure you vary your type and frequency of celebrations so they don't become predictable. Verbal and physical celebrations cost you little except your time, and can be given out with whatever abundance your time and energy allows. Monetary celebrations will be restricted by your budget. However, since all celebrations increase production, monetary celebrations are an investment where the more you share, the more you get in return.

CHECKING FOR UNDERSTANDING

1. Some period of celebration is important after reaching stated goals.   T   F

2. Rewards are closely associated with the idea of punishment.   T   F

3. The child in you can wait until you have successfully completed the whole project before celebrating.   T   F

4. It is important to vary your celebrations so that they appeal to your Parent, Adult, and Child ego states.   T   F

5. It is important to enjoy short celebrations as well as major ones.   T   F

6. Celebrations don't have to cost money.   T   F

7. Celebrating the accomplishment of sales activity on the way to your goal is as important as celebrating the accomplishment of the total goal.   T   F

8. It isn't important to keep track of your successes.   T   F

9. Celebrating produces feelings that in- T   F
   crease the energy in your magnetic energy field.

Answers

1. T   6. T

2. T   7. T

3. F   8. F

4. T   9. T

5. T

DECIDING ON THE GUIDELINES FOR YOUR CELEBRATIONS

Directions: The first step in celebrating your successes is to determine the guidelines for your celebrations. Use the following questions to help you decide your personal preferences. List them on a separate sheet of paper.

1. How often will you celebrate?
2. How much money will you set aside in your budget for celebrations for the month?
3. What sales-related activity will you acknowledge with a celebration?

Examples: Making the number of telephone calls you agreed to do, making the number of presentations you agreed to do, keeping a sale together that looked like it was going to fall apart, finding just the right item for your customer, learning a new close, etc.

- List the steps involved in your line of sales.
- List the steps involved in reaching your weekly, monthly, quarterly, and yearly sales goals. At what points will you celebrate and how?

4. What management activity will you acknowledge with a celebration?

Examples: Recruiting a certain number of people, reaching company quotas, a new recruit's first sale, helping a salesperson salvage a "lost" sale, etc.

- List the steps involved in recruiting, training, and managing your staff. At what points will you celebrate and how?

DECIDING WHAT CELEBRATIONS SPUR YOU ON

Directions: The familiar saying, "Different strokes for different folks" applies in deciding what celebrations spur you on to greater achievement. What motivates others may not work for you and vice versa. Decide what feels like a celebration for you, and custom-tailor your celebrations to fit your own needs. As you think of activities, list them on a separate sheet of paper.

1. What do you do that is especially meaningful to you? Dinner out? A day at the races? A day at the beach? Hang-gliding? Reading your favorite book for two hours? Going to a seminar to learn a new sales technique? (Be sure to include things that are meaningful to your Parent, Adult, and Child.)
2. What are some five-minute celebrations you can do?

Examples: call a friend and share your results, go for a walk and enjoy the scenery, read one page of jokes, write a short note to a friend in another city, listen to a song on a cassette, etc.

Directions: Once you have a general list of celebrations, categorize them according to the ego state they would satisfy.

1. Write all the celebrations that would delight or satisfy the Child in you on one page.
2. Write all the celebrations that would delight or satisfy the Adult in you on one page.
3. Write all the celebrations that would delight or satisfy the Parent in you on one page.

Sometimes you find a celebration that satisfies all three ego states at the same time such as learning a new aerobics routine. Your Parent is happy that you are taking care of your body, your Adult enjoys mastering the new routine, and your Child has fun dancing to the music. Write all the celebrations that would delight or satisfy the Parent, Adult and Child in you on one page.

Your lists of celebrations serve three purposes. First, they provide you with an instant source of fun things to do when you have cause for celebration. Second, they serve as motivation for you as you think about the exciting things in store as you reach your goals. Third, the lists serve to remind you to rotate your celebrations so that all ego states have a chance to enjoy your successes.

Allow yourself to be flexible in your celebrations. You may plan ahead of time to do "x" to celebrate, only to discover when the day arrives that you really want to do "y." Go with what feels right to you at the moment, and fully enjoy celebrating your successes!

POSITIVE AFFIRMATIONS

Directions: Repeat these affirmations on a daily basis to internalize the principles of your subconscious and hasten the achievement of your desired results.

1. I enjoy celebrating my successes on a regular basis.
2. I vary my celebrations to satisfy the Parent, Adult, and Child within me.
3. I celebrate the intermediate steps necessary to reach my major goals.
4. I physically enthuse about my successes which increases the intensity of the energy in my magnetic energy field.
5. I love to talk about my successes, because my energy field automatically brings me more of what I'm talking about.

THE
SECRETS
OF
SUPERSELLING

Secret Nine

When There is a Delay, Take Inventory

Identifying Where You Settle for Less Than You Really
  Want
Identifying past and Present Forms of Punishment
Positive Affirmations

PREVIEW OF SECRET NINE

WHEN THERE IS A DELAY, TAKE INVENTORY

There are times after you program your subconscious, that you achieve your sales goals easily and quickly. There are other times when you feel stuck and it seems you may never reach your goal. This usually means you have unconscious blocks to reaching your objective. In Secret Nine, you learn to take inventory of your subconscious and to identify the blocks that are causing your delay. Dissolving them (which you will learn to do in Secret Ten) is the final step in reaching your goal.

WHEN THERE IS A DELAY, TAKE INVENTORY

DEALING WITH OBSTACLES

You have read this book and carefully followed the steps as outlined in the first eight Secrets. If you have not yet reached your goal, you may find yourself doubting the methods presented here, or worse yet, doubting your ability to apply the techniques successfully.

Perhaps you have not had enough time to reach your goal. If this is the case, additional time is all you need. On the other hand, if there is truly a delay in reaching your goal, it simply means there are obstacles in your subconscious that need to be removed so you can go on to achieve your chosen result.

Identifying the obstacles or blocks that are causing your delay is the first step in removing them. Dissolving them (which you will learn to do in secret Ten) is the final step in using your marvelous subconscious to get exactly what you want!

THE OBSTACLE OF COMPARING

Comparing yourself to others can result in your creating an unconscious negative goal. In order to reach your desired result, this negative goal must be dissolved.

Don't Compare and Come Up Short

Example: Rosemary is a salesperson whose desire was to get a $6,000 commission check in one month. She knew it was possible, for she saw others in her office receive $6,000 commissions.

Eventually, Rosemary realized that each time she saw someone else get a "big check," she thought, "What's different about me? Why don't I receive $6,000 checks?" As she compared herself to others, she had these thoughts:

About Herself:

1. "I don't get big checks."
2. "My deals fall through."
3. "I work harder than they do and get less money.'"
4. "I don't have big sales."
5. "I'm sad, (mad, scared, jealous, frustrated, etc.)."
6. "I don't have as much money as I want and need."
7. "I'm not as rich as they are."

About Others:

1. "They get big checks."
2. "Their deals close."
3. "They work less than I do and get more money."
4. "They have big sales."
5. "They're happy."
6. "They have more money than they need."
7. "They're rich."

As Rosemary experienced these thoughts, she had feelings of sadness, helplessness, anger, and fear. Because she is a strong, determined person, she also had thoughts of, "No matter how tough it is, I don't give up!"

Fueled by determination to succeed, she insisted she was going to get ahead in sales. The problem came from her insistence on achieving a positive outcome, while thinking negative thoughts, and feeling upset from comparing herself with others.

Remember, when there is a conflict, your subconscious acts on your dominant beliefs and feelings. What Rosemary didn't understand was that she believed the negative *more* than she believed the positive. As a result, she was creating the following:

No $6,000 check
Deals falling through
Working hard for little money
No big sale
Feeling sad, mad, scared. . . .
Not as rich as others

Your subconscious accepts anything you repeat over and over with strong feeling as a goal you want to achieve. Your magnetic energy field then draws to you exactly what you picture and talk about, and pushes away anything different.

As Rosemary processed this situation in the Secrets of Superselling workshop, she was instructed to write positive denials and affirmations such as:

1. "I'm not different from other salespeople who receive big checks. I'm just like them."

2. "I no longer say I don't have big sales. I do have big sales."

3. "It's not true that my deals fall through. They all close."

4. "I don't believe I don't have enough money. I have more money than I need."

5. "I'm not sad, mad, and scared any longer. I'm happy and rich."

6. "I forgive myself for unknowingly creating 'no big sales.' I create big ones."

7. "I work smart, and get lots of money. I have several big sales, and receive $6,000 monthly commission checks just like the others."

Rosemary was also instructed to get her picture taken with the salespeople in her office who had received checks of $6,000 or more. Under the picture she was to write, "I'm one of them. I get $6,000 checks, too."

After reading her positive denials and affirmations, viewing her pictures regularly, and doing the activities to dissolve energy blocks, her income started increasing. She reached the $6,000 mark through her persistence and dedication to reaching her goal.

THE OBSTACLE OF LANGUAGE

Sometimes you experience a delay when you unknowingly program your subconscious with incorrect language. In this section you will learn how the language you use can become an obstacle to achieving your goal.

When You Need, You Don't Get

Example: Tom is a real estate agent who did very well in his business until he changed companies. He then experienced a lull in selling. For several months, he kept telling his friends, family and colleagues how he needed a sale. He asked everyone the same question: "Do you want to buy a house? I need a sale." If you look up the word need in the dictionary, you discover that it means "lack of." When you say, "I need a sale," you are actually saying, "I lack a sale."

Your subconscious does not think, "Oh, Tom said 'need' . . . that means lack. I know he doesn't want me to create the lack of a sale for him. He just used the wrong word. He really means 'have', so I'll go ahead and create a sale for him." Your subconscious takes you literally and precisely, and gives you exactly what you say you want.

Remember, Confucius said the first thing he would do if he were made Emperor of China would be to re-establish the precise meaning of words. In the *Secrets of Superselling*, Tom was helped to understand that he was creating "no sales" because of what he was saying, feeling, and picturing in his mind.

As long as he kept declaring, "I need a sale," he had no sales. His subconscious gave him exactly what he repeated over and over . . . a need for sales. Once he learned what was causing his situation, he quickly changed his tune by sitting down and making the following list of the thoughts he was having about his career.

1. "I made the National Home Builders Association Million Dollar Club last year."

2. "I want to make the Million Dollar Club for my county."
3. "If I had listings, I could turn them into sales."
4. "I changed companies, and left all my listings with my old company. I have no listings."
5. "It is the middle of December, and I don't have much time left this year to makes sales."
6. "It's the holiday season and people don't want to be bothered by agents."

The next thing Tom did was to write positive denials and affirmations such as, "It's not true that I can't get listings just because it is the holidays. I get listings just as easily now as any other time." He stopped feeling the lack of listings, and got the feeling of having both listings and sales. In the last ten days of December, when people were busy celebrating the holidays, Tom got ten listings. Instead of trying to get individual listings, he met with a builder and listed ten of his homes in one subdivision. Within two months, he had sold five of the ten homes.

Need Means Lack

Let's look at additional cases of "need." If you are a sales manager and keep saying, "I need some really good producers," you are actually saying, "I lack some really good producers." This could result in top producers leaving and going to another company. Your energy field must push away from you anything that is different from what you declare to be true. Therefore, really good producers can't stay with you or be drawn to you when you keep saying you don't have them.

If your car is not the greatest, and you keep thinking, "I need a good car," you are really saying, "I lack a good car." Your subconscious will do whatever it takes to keep you needing and lacking a good car. You'll find you are calling on people who are not good prospects. You'll be busy, but you won't be selling. Therefore, you won't earn enough money to get your new car.

If you *think* you can make your sales quota, but you *feel* like you really *need* to make your sales quota, you will fall short of your goal. This happens because feelings carry more weight with your subconscious than thoughts. When there is a difference between what you think and what you feel, your subconscious produces what you are feeling rather than what you are thinking.

> *Any time you hear yourself saying or thinking,*
> *"I need . . ." blow the whistle, ring the bells, and*
> *make sure you move from needing what you*
> *have identified as a lack in your life, to feeling*
> *like that lack is satisfied.*

The authors do not mean to give the impression that it is wrong to ever say, "I need." It is always necessary to discover what your needs are, so you can set goals. However, it is crucial that your next step is to erase the thought of need from your mind and the feeling of lack from your emotions. Then, see yourself with the need satisfied, and get the good feeling of already having what you want. This results in the successful achievement of your goal.

THE OBSTACLE OF TOO LITTLE CREATIVITY

At times you try to achieve goals by relying primarily on logic and techniques you have learned from others. This can become a block to reaching your goal, which might be cleared up by simply allowing your creativity to flourish. Creative thinking may then show you a new way to reach your desired destination. This section will help you open the doors to your own increased creativity.

Give Your Creativity A Boost

You have no choice as to whether or not you will use your subconscious. You are always using this powerful, creative instrument to create your reality. You are always programming your subconscious through what you are doing, seeing, feeling, and thinking.

Let's say Dave shows you a plaque he received for selling a

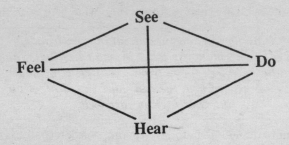

certain amount. (See) You hold the plaque. (Do) Desire wells up in you to receive that award, too. (Feel) In your mind you start planning how you can reach that level of production. (Hear) You get your picture taken holding that plaque. (Do) You see yourself standing on the stage receiving a plaque just like Dave's. (See . . . in your imagination) You continue seeing, feeling, hearing, and doing until the plaque is yours!

Many times you achieve your goals easily, but sometimes there is a delay in reaching a goal. The delay may be eliminated by tapping into your creativity. Just as goals are achieved through seeing, feeling, hearing, and doing, creativity is enhanced and triggered through the same avenues.

What Opens the Door to Your Creativity?

It is possible to get in touch with your creativity through any of four doors.

SEEING
It could be that visually staring at a picture of your completed project, will open the floodgate of your creativity. It is also possible that by sitting quietly and focusing your eyes on a flower, tree, or other object, your creative mind will share its wonderful ideas with you.

HEARING
For some people, the activity of hearing something starts them on the path to tuning into their creative abilities. It may be the

sound of voices, music, nature, or even machinery. Many people do their best creative ventures while listening to the hum of a typewriter, the washing machine, the electrical tools in the shop, or other sounds.

DOING

If this is the way to tap into your creativity, you will function well by being physically involved with something. Your activities might be sitting at your typewriter or piano in a state of relaxed expectancy, idly strumming a guitar, doodling with your pencil, holding a hammer along with some wood and nails, draping some fabric over your body in different ways, or any other activities that you use to express your creative talent. You may be walking, riding in your car, sitting with a pencil and paper so you can begin writing ideas down, and so on.

FEELING

You may find that fully experiencing your emotions as you see, do, and hear, opens the door to your own unique creativity. You don't need to do anything special to get into your feelings. Simply allow yourself to experience your feelings as you play sports, watch television, do sales presentations, etc.

SOME OF EACH

You may find that a combination of all four works wonders for you. It is possible that your ideal setting for creativity might look like this: You take a walk along the beach, feeling the water rush over your feet while the sand squishes between your toes. The sound of the waves is music to your ears; you watch the sun slowly sink into the horizon. When you return to your chair, you play a piece of music on your tape recorder, and a wonderful feeling of peace and serenity floods through your body.

Suddenly, you get an idea that solves a problem you've been puzzling over for some time, or you get an idea for a poem, a design for a building, a new way to prospect for clients, or a new way to close sales. Once you discover what opens the door to your creativity, you can recreate that sequence of events whenever you wish.

Creativity Boosters

Another crucial ingredient in creativity is relaxation of mind and body. The following are some activities that induce relaxation.

1. Walking or lying on the beach.
2. Sitting by a waterfall.
3. Walking in a peaceful forest or desert.
4. Gardening.
5. Meditation.
6. Mild physical exercise.
7. Baths and showers.
8. Driving in the car on a peaceful road.

The power of water to help you tap into increased creativity is evidenced in the story of Archimedes, who was asked by King Hiero II of Syracuse whether the king's crown was made of solid gold or an alloy of gold and silver. As Archimedes was taking his bath, he came up with the idea of immersing the crown in water. If it were pure gold, it would displace less water than if it were an alloy.

As we have said, people often solve problems easier when they are near sources of water. One explanation for this is that the water gives off negative ions which increase creativity. Another source of negative ions is plants. While they are decorative in the home or office, they appear to serve the additional purpose of helping people be more creative.

In addition to relaxation, an increase in circulation is helpful. This can be achieved through mild physical exercise which brings more blood to your brain, giving it more oxygen and biochemical nutrients. If you have been stumped about a situation, or just find that you are bored with an academic activity, mild exercise may get your creative juices flowing once more.

**"True happiness lies in the joy of achievement
and the thrill of creative effort."**
Franklin Roosevelt

THE OBSTACLE OF HAVING LOST PEOPLE OR THINGS

In this section you will learn how holding on to negative feelings about past experiences causes those same experiences to be repeated. In Secret Ten, you will learn how to dissolve this negative energy so that you no longer repeat the losses.

Loss Brings More Loss

Once thoughts and feelings are accepted by your subconscious, a magnetic energy field is created around you. As we've mentioned in several previous secrets, this energy field must draw to you whatever you describe and push away from you anything different from what you describe.

It has been found that we absorb feelings from other people much like a sponge soaks up water. Children take on the feelings of others without realizing it. As we said earlier, there is a stage of development when the child cannot tell the difference between him or herself and others. If mother is hungry, the child wants to eat. If mother is angry, the child yells and throws his or her toys. (The child acts out the feelings of father and other significant people also.)

The process of soaking up other people's feelings continues throughout your life. Feelings from scenes that are heavily charged with emotion sometimes get stuck in your energy field. They stay there and reproduce the negative consequences until they are re-experienced and dissolved. A feeling of loss lodged deep in your subconscious will bring more loss until you dissolve those thoughts and feelings from your magnetic energy field.

Example: Loss Bringing More Loss Joann entered into a marriage when she was very young. It soon ended in divorce leaving her to raise her son by herself. She did very well financially in sales and bought a lovely home. Many years later she fell in love and remarried. Her husband and his children from a previous marriage moved into her established home. Through some unfortunate circumstances, he had no income, and was unable to find work. She supported the family as long as she could. However, her income was not enough to support both herself and her increased family. Eventually, the second marriage broke up, and she was left with a severely damaged credit rating. Finally, she lost her home.

The financial troubles had been going on for almost three years when Joann consulted one of the authors in hopes of clearing up the situation. During the process, Joann realized that she had experienced a number of losses when she was growing up that had a similar pattern to the loss she was dealing with currently.

The Process of Loss Bringing More Loss

When Joann was three years old, she had something she loved. (Cat) There was a problem. (Cat scratched her.) She lost what she loved because of something someone else did. (Dad got rid of the cat.)

When Joann was eleven, she had someone she liked very much. (Best friend.) There was a problem. (She had to move away from this friend.) She lost this close friendship, because of something someone else did. (Father's company transferred him to another city.)

Because of these and similar experiences, Joann came to this conclusion: "I lose what I love and that causes me pain."

Let's look now at the similarities in the situation she was experiencing as an adult. She loved her second husband, but couldn't make ends meet with the increased financial burden. She lost the home she was so proud of, and her excellent credit rating was damaged because of something someone else did. The situation may look different at first, but it is the very same process.

She had something she loved. (Home, husband, good credit rating.) There was a problem. (She couldn't meet the increased financial burden.) She lost what she loved because of what someone else did. (Husband added to the financial burden, and didn't add to the income. She lost the home, husband, and good credit rating.)

During the time they were together, she suffered much emotional pain. She loved him, but also resented his not helping financially. After the breakup, she continued to suffer much emotional pain as she dealt with creditors and finally lost her home.

Joann˜ was instructed to do the following to dissolve this situation from her energy field.

1. Write daily for at least thirty days: "What I love no longer causes me pain. I don't lose what I love anymore."
2. Feel her sadness, rage, anger, and hurt connected with losing the cat, her friend, her husband, her home, and good credit rating.
3. Visualize herself forgiving her father for being responsible for her losses as a child.
4. Visualize herself forgiving her second husband for adding to the financial burden by not bringing in any money.
5. Visualize forgiving herself for having gotten involved with her second husband.
6. Dissolve feelings of sadness, rage, anger, and hurt by writing and saying on a daily basis, "I am not mad at James or myself anymore. I'm not afraid to love again. Nothing I love causes me pain anymore. I'm no longer a victim of someone else's decisions."

Once the feeling of loss was dissolved, Joann's subconscious was able to use this energy in the achievement of her sales goals.

THE OBSTACLE OF ENERGY BLOCKS

In this section, you will learn a technique to identify what is blocking your achievement on an energy level. By releasing the blocked energy, you have more power to achieve your goal.

Discovering Unwanted Energy Patterns

John James, a transactional analyst, developed a procedure called John James Game Plan which is helpful in discovering unwanted energy patterns. It does this by allowing you to see the pattern into which your energy has been formed. Once you see the pattern, you know what steps to take to free your energy so it can be used in achieving new goals.

The first step in James' game plan is to list the events in a situation you'd like to stop experiencing. List them in the order in which they occur, using as few words as possible. Write them in simple terms, as if you were telling them to a five-year old. Include the feelings you have about the experience as well.

Example:
Step 1. List the events and feelings:
I get a new client.
I have more money than I need.
I feel good.
I lose an old client.
I'm back to making ends meet.
I feel bad.
I get mad.
I get another new client.
(The cycle is repeated over and over.)

Step 2. Reduce the information to even fewer words:
Get new client.
Have excess money.
Feel good.
Lose old client.
Just enough money.
Feel bad.
Get mad.
Get new client.

Step 3. Reduce it again:
Get.
Have excess.
Feel good.
Lose.
Feel bad.
Get mad.
Get more.

When it is simplified, you see a general pattern. In this case it is: "I want, I get, I feel good. I lose what I get and feel bad. I get mad and get more, which I lose again."

When you look past the specific content of getting a new client and losing an old one, you see the person in replaying a process that happens often while growing up. As babies crawl around, they find wonderful new items, and feel good until an adult comes along and takes the new treasures away. Then babies feel bad. Often they cry, and some go so far as to have a temper tantrum before going on to something new. These patterns often continue throughout childhood. Through repeated experiences, beliefs such as the following are developed. "I feel bad after I feel good." "I have to get mad to get what I want." These beliefs cause the person to continue to have the experiences of feeling bad after feeling good and getting mad before getting what he or she wants. As long as the thoughts and feelings exist in the subconscious, the magnetic energy field will continue to attract more of the same experiences.

Step 4. Design positive denials and affirmations to dissolve the unwanted pattern such as:

- "I no longer lose an old client when I gain a new one. I keep old ones and gain new ones."
- "It's not true that I can't have more than just enough to get by. I deserve to have more money than I need."
- "I no longer feel bad after I feel good. I feel good all the time."

There is no magic number of repetitions that guarantee acceptance by your subconscious. Sometimes several repetitions are enough. Sometimes many repetitions are needed. Continue your positive denials and affirmations until the negative results no longer happen in your life. (See Secret Ten for additional steps in dissolving energy patterns.)

THE OBSTACLE OF FEELING LIKE YOU DON'T DESERVE WHAT YOU WANT

Along with the skills needed to reach your goals, you must feel that you deserve to have what you want. In this section, you learn where some of your "I don't deserve it" feelings originated, and what to do about them.

In *Think & Grow Rich*, Napoleon Hill writes that the subconscious is a field of consciousness in which every impression reaching the objective mind from sight, taste, smell, touch, and hearing is classified and recorded. Let's look at how some of these impressions affect your feeling of deserving.

As a child you sometimes experienced punishment and deprivation of privileges for "wrong-doings."

1. You spilled your milk and were sent to your room.
2. In school you talked at the wrong time, so you couldn't go out for recess, and had to stay in the classroom alone.
3. At home you fought with your sister and couldn't watch TV for two weeks.

Your Left Brain Deals with the Content of the Situations:

1. Spilled milk . . . time out.
2. Talked . . . missed recess.
3. Fought . . . couldn't watch TV.

From the many details, you form the bigger picture, and draw conclusions. One conclusion you might draw is, "When you do something wrong, you must pay by being deprived of something that gives you pleasure."

You then react to this judgment with feelings of anger, sadness, loss, fear, frustration, desire for revenge, and so forth.

Pictures and thoughts get reviewed over and over in your mind, just as television stations present reruns of shows. As you review these pictures, you make decisions for yourself as to how much you deserve, based on the wrong-doings along with your good deeds.

Your level of deserving can be thought of as your line of credit at the bank. When applying for a line of credit, the banker looks at your assets, income, and liabilities. The decision is then made as to how high your credit line is to be.

Upon exceeding your line of credit, you are not allowed any more money, until you have reduced your indebtedness. It is the same with your level of deserving. Once you exceed your own predetermined limits, your internal monitoring system does something to bring things back into line.

Let's say you have gotten new clothes, a better job, and a nicer car. Your Conscious Assessment:

You got too much. You exceeded your limit. You may feel guilty and believe you must pay by being deprived of something that gives you pleasure. Your subconscious now has the task of creatively finding a way to deprive you of something that you enjoy. In this case, the "punishments" might look like this:

1. You gain weight and are temporarily deprived of your new clothes.

2. You get sick and can't go on the trip you've been planning.

3. A deal you thought was a sure thing suddenly falls through.

After a period of time of being deprived, you go on a diet, reduce your weight, and wear your clothes again. You get well and plan another trip. You work out the kinks in the deal, and it finally goes through.

In order to better understand how some people deal with the process of punishment and levels of deserving, let's look at transactional analysis.

TRANSACTIONAL ANALYSIS: A HELPFUL MODEL FOR UNDERSTANDING BEHAVIOR

Some people have internal dialogues going on in their heads all the time. Much of the talking happens without their consciously hearing any of the thoughts. The internal negative Parent says things like, "You've done lots of things 'wrong.' You don't deserve whatever it is you want, and you can't have it." The compliant Child responds with, "You're right . . . but I'm mad and sad." A person may live out his or her life submitting to this limit.

Another person may hear the same thoughts and react as a spiteful, compliant Child. "I'm mad. I hate people who have what I want. If I can't have what I want, you can't have what you want either."

This person gets into revenge, but is not conscious of doing so. He or she breaks things or messes up projects. It all looks accidental. There is much penitence, and the person continually apologizes and feels sorry.

The punitive part of a person is the first to be put to sleep with alcohol. Sometimes this person will drink alcohol to help him or herself avoid acting out the spiteful feelings. (The authors are not suggesting that all people who drink do so to subdue spiteful feelings,for this is not true.)

For someone else, the hopeless compliant Child may respond, "I feel so hopeless and helpless. I don't know how I'll ever get what I want." This person is often listless and it's hard for him or her to get going.

There are times when a person will go through several of these phases.

1. A person wants something.
2. The internal Parent says "no."
3. The internal Child says, "I'm mad."
4. The person may have a drink or two and switch from feeling mad to sad, hopeless, and helpless.

5. The internal Child may beg and plead with the internal Parent for hours or days without your being consciously aware of the process.

Other people react differently. When the internal Parent says no, the internal rebellious Child says, "I don't care what you say. I'm getting what I want anyway!" This person has a lot of anger from both the negative internal Parent and Child. He or she is likely to depend on stimulants of some sort to get that extra boost of energy needed to do daily tasks. In spite of all obstacles, this person gets what is wanted. However, the success is short-lived. Once the objective is reached, the negative internal Parent comes on with renewed vigor. "I told you this was not allowed! You don't deserve this much. You have to pay by doing without something that gives you pleasure."

The internal compliant Child agrees, "You're right, I do feel guilty." The stage is now set for this person to pay in some way.

Feel Good—Feel Bad

With each of these sequences, the person first feels good while choosing what is wanted, and imagining the pleasure of the chosen item. The person may then feel bad when told "no." In the case of the rebellious Child going for it anyway, the person doesn't feel bad until the goal has been achieved, and the compliant Child then agrees with the negative internal Parent. At this point, something gets taken away and the person feels bad. Sometimes this process is handled by the person deciding to give in, give up, and not go for very much anymore. The feeling is, "What's the point of going for it and getting it if it's going to be taken away?" The pain of losing what he or she once had is so great, the person would rather do without completely. However, other people are willing to bear the pain of losing what was gained. They believe the pain of not having at all is worse than having and then losing.

How the "Goodies" May Get Taken Away

It is possible for you to take things away from yourself without anyone else's help. Here are some examples:

1. You land a big contract because your bid is so low. You make no profit and sometimes even lose money on deals because of such low bids.
2. You are a good achiever. You spend much time in between accomplishments straightening out messes, looking for lost objects, fumbling through mounds of paperwork looking for needed bits of information, etc.
3. A streak of "bad luck" follows a promotion and increased income. You lose a contact lens, break the heel of a shoe, have an accident with the car, and on it goes.

Finally you say, "Stop, it can't get any worse than it is now. It's bound to get better!" These declarations along with the feeling energy generated by them stop the "loss," and things start getting better.

At times a person who feels he or she has too much teams up with a person who feels spiteful from not being able to get what is wanted. Let's look at some examples of this type of "teamwork."

1. A salesperson closes many deals. The secretary then sends mail out late, doesn't get phone messages down correctly, and so forth. He or she then spends time fixing mistakes instead of selling.
2. The husband makes a higher income and buys a nicer car. The wife or teenager has an accident. Part of the increased profit goes to repair the damaged car.
3. The boss may sell big contracts. However, much of the profit goes into fixing messes created by employees who have broken or lost equipment and done jobs that don't measure up to the company's standards.

THE OBSTACLE OF FEELING LESS THAN OR BETTER THAN

In this section, you learn how the life positions of "I'm OK—You're not," or "I'm not OK—You Are," can get in the way of your getting what you want. You'll also see how "I'm OK—You're OK," is a win-win way to play the game of life.

I'm OK—You're OK

The feelings you have about yourself and others can have a major impact on your selling. Many of these feelings come from unconscious positions you take about yourself and others that may be buried in your subconscious. These life positions have an effect on how you interact with people.

Frank Ernst, Jr. M.D., practitioner of transactional analysis, developed a way of classifying the outcomes of the events in your life. The four possible life positions from which people operate are as follows: Get-On-With, Get-Away-From, Get-Rid-Of and Get-Nowhere-With. As you learn to recognize the life positions from which you and others operate, you are able to communicate more effectively to get the result you want.

Let's look at the four life positions and how people feel in each one.

1. I'm OK-You're OK—Let's Get On With It!

The best position to come from in all transactions is I'm OK—You're OK. In this position you feel good about yourself, and the people with whom you deal. You expect situations to work out positively and this comes across to others. You spend, use, and invest time to everyone's best advantage.

It is possible for you to maintain an I'm OK-You're OK position even when things aren't going well. Perhaps you are working on a deal where you need additional data (which someone neglected to supply to you) before you can move ahead with the sale. In this position, you continue to feel good about yourself and the person who did not supply the data, and get on with other parts of the deal. The point here is that the I'm OK-You're OK position is based on an attitude about life . . . not on the condition that everything goes smoothly in each transaction.

2. I'm Not OK-You're OK—I Have to Get Away From You.

In this position, you may feel like "I'm not OK as a salesperson because I don't know enough closing techniques, but you're OK as a prospect. Since this is a Get-Away-From position, you will spend most of your time trying to get away from your prospects. You will cut sales presentations to a minimum, and leave as soon as possible, before they find out just how few closing techniques you have. When you are complimented, you very likely will not fully accept the compliment. How can a not-OK person believe wonderful things about him or herself?

3. I'm OK-You're Not OK—I Have to Get Rid Of You.

When coming from this Get-Rid-Of position, you feel good about yourself, but view the prospect or customer as not OK. You have a tendency to look for their faults. This comes across to the prospect, and because they are feeling, "I'm not OK," they want to Get-Away-From you as quickly as possible. You may be rude, or not spend the necessary time with them. Another possibility is that you have the attitude of "I'm OK-You're not . . . but you could be if you would buy my product." Many sales can be made with this attitude, but there is a high rate of returns. Even when the customer keeps the item, there is very little repeat business.

4. I'm Not OK-You're Not OK—We Are Stuck With Each Other in a "No Win" Situation.

Getting stuck in the I'm not OK-You're not OK position is very uncomfortable and can lead to sales slumps. You feel that you are not OK because you can't get yourself straightened out and you feel that the customers or prospects are not OK because they are not buying from you. If this position continues, you will probably change jobs. However, if you believe you have to stick with this job, you feel cornered and may resign yourself to live out your "sentence" in misery, and just hope it doesn't get absolutely unbearable. You may feel defeated.

You endure jobs you don't like, put up with marriages you hate, and so on because you believe, "I'm not OK because . . . and You're not OK because. . . ." This position stifles problem solving, because you feel there is no way out.

Application to Selling

With an I'm OK-You're OK position, it's easy to prospect, set appointments, call on people, and make sales. You make friends easily as well. People get the idea that you feel good about yourself, and like them, too. Think how different your attitude and activity is if you are functioning from the position of I'm not OK-You're OK. From this position, it's hard to get the courage to make phone calls, set appointments, and call on potential clients or buyers since most of your energy is tied up in getting away from people as soon as possible.

If you are functioning from the I'm OK-You're not OK position, you very likely will have little patience with the people you are selling. They will feel somewhat intimidated when on the receiving end of an I'm OK-You're not encounter. They buy, believing consciously or unconsciously they need to do this to become OK. Some cancelled deals come about from selling from this position.

Trying to sell from an I'm not OK-You're not OK position is just about impossible. You don't feel good about yourself, because you see yourself as a poor closer, poor prospector, not good on the telephone, etc. You don't feel good about others, because you are sure they won't want your product, or the ones who want it won't get financing, etc.

Once you get into this position, the job becomes not OK, and the company is likewise not OK. Your family even slips in favor, because they didn't help you like Henry's family helped him . . . and the list goes on and on.

> *No matter what the circumstances, any selling slump can be impacted positively by dissolving accumulated negative energy, and functioning once more from a position of I'm OK-You're OK.*

THE OBSTACLE OF FEELING TRAPPED

There are times when you feel trapped . . . damned if you do, and damned if you don't. In this section you learn to spring the "corner" trap that keeps you from reaching the goals you've chosen.

It's OK to Leave the Corner

Sometimes when you have not yet reached your goal, you feel as if you are trapped in a corner. A corner is any situation in which you think you will lose no matter what you do. It's the, "damned if I do, damned if I don't" syndrome.

Many years ago, schoolteachers put children who misbehaved in the corner. The student was instructed to sit there, face the wall, and not get up until the teacher gave permission to do so. As the child sat looking at the wall, there was nowhere to go, and no way out until someone else said he or she could leave.

Even now as adults, we sometimes find ourselves in a corner emotionally and psychologically. We then feel trapped, seeing no way out. Very often the judgments and feelings responsible for our being in the corner are not in our conscious awareness. This makes it doubly hard for us to give ourselves permission to leave the corner.

Before considering how we can get ourselves out of the corner trap, let's see how we got there in the first place. Using the TA model, let's look at two examples of feeling cornered.

Example: To Be or Not To Be a Salesman John had wanted to be a salesman for as long as he could remember. Even while he was in school, he had made pocket money buying and selling things to friends for a profit. He learned quite early that you could work for a few dollars an hour, or you could make the same amount or more in minutes through selling. The creativity, challenge, and payoff of selling excited him and became a strong part of his Child ego state.

John's mother and father felt differently about salespeople. They were midwestern farmers who toiled long, hard hours for their money. They felt that getting money fast and easy was somehow wrong, even though it was done legitimately. They were not bashful about telling him this along with their idea that most salesmen were cheats and liars. These messages from his parents became a strong, although unconscious, part of his Parent ego state.

Despite his parents' protests, John went on to fulfill his dream and was soon the top salesman in his company. Then something happened. It began taking him longer and longer to close each sale. The easy sales that had been his trademark grew fewer and fewer.

John was in the corner, but didn't know it. His Child ego state had the desire to be a top salesman. It still loved the challenge of making money quickly and easily. However, his Parent ego state didn't want him to be a salesman at all.

Using the TA model, the dialogue between John's Parent and Child ego states went something like the following:

Parent: "You're a salesperson. You're bad. You are making money too fast and easy."

Child: "I'm sorry. I will work harder so I'm worthy of the money I make."

Parent: "Working hard won't help. Salespeople are cheats and liars. Get a respectable job!"

Child: "But I like being a salesperson. I don't want to have to work at something I don't like!"

John felt cornered because if he sold, he was bad, and if he did something else, he got mad. Selling was not an honorable profession in his family's eyes, and making the same income some other way was too hard in his opinion. As long as this internal struggle continued, John would be unhappy no matter what he did.

Example: How Do You Get Started? Here you will see how your Child ego state can feel cornered without any Parent ego state input.

Child: "Gee, I want to do well in this new sales position, but I don't see how I can! To do well, you have to have referrals. I feel stuck! I can't get sales because I don't have referrals and I can't get referrals, because I haven't had any sales! How do you get started in this business?"

From this dialogue, you see how the Child ego state created the corner through the belief that to get sales you must first have referrals and to get referrals you must first have sales.

Getting Out of the Corner

The first step in getting out of the corner is to realize that you are there. Sometimes this awareness comes as a feeling of being trapped or immobilized without any conscious thoughts of the problem or situation.

Once you are aware of feeling cornered, think about goals you have been trying to reach. Begin by analyzing where you are with each goal. When you find a place where you seem to be "spinning your wheels" and getting nowhere, jot down the obstacles you think are keeping you from reaching that goal. As you continue to list obstacles, you will notice that two of the obstacles are related to each other such as needing referrals to get sales and needing sales to get referrals. These related obstacles form the sides of the corner. After you have identified the two sides of the corner, do some brainstorming on how you can deal with each obstacle. In the example of needing both sales and referrals at the same time, you might come up with the idea of talking to someone who is doing very well in your business in order to find out how he or she got started. You could then follow those same strategies.

Another action step in getting out of the corner is to move from a position of I'm not OK-You're not OK, which goes along with feeling cornered, to I'm OK-You're OK. To do this, you forgive yourself and others for whatever has happened in the past. You unconditionally accept yourself, others, and what is happening in your life. (See Secret Ten to learn how to dissolve any negative feelings you may have about what has happened in the past.)

PREVENT SLUMPS AFTER MAJOR ACCOMPLISHMENTS

It's common for salespeople to have a major accomplishment, followed by a period of no sales. The major accomplishment might be:

1. Becoming agent of the month.
2. Becoming salesperson of the year.
3. Making the biggest sale in the office's history.
4. Making sales easier and quicker than usual.
5. Earning more money in one day than ever earned before.

Here are three possible causes of sales slumps.

1. Sometimes after you make a big sale, or are given a sales honor, you start thinking and saying, "I'll never be able to make that big a sale or make top salesperson again, etc." Or, if a day or two goes by with few sales, you think, "I'm not doing as well as I did last month. I don't know what is wrong with me!" You then start trying to figure out what is wrong.

As you keep looking for the reasons you are not producing, you may be unknowingly programming the sales slump itself.

When you think, "I'm not doing as well," over and over, the goal of not doing well is inadvertantly created in your subconscious. Not doing as well now becomes your new goal. Remember, thoughts and feelings repeated over and over become accepted by your subconscious as goals to be achieved.

2. Another reason for there being a slow period following a bigger-than-usual accomplishment is that you need time to enthuse and rest. If you continue business as usual, you find yourself moving a little slower, and a voice in your head says, "You're not working. How do you expect to put bread and butter on the table?" You start affirming, "Gosh, I'm not selling. I won't be able to make ends meet!" As you think this over and over, it becomes a self-fulfilling prophecy, and you find yourself in a sales slump. Instead of getting caught up in worrying about the lack of production, you need guilt-free time to rest and celebrate. Then you can return to work refreshed and raring to go!

3. Sometimes, the reason production stops after a bigger-than-usual accomplishment is that you simply forget to program the next goal. Think about this in terms of baking a cake. Once the cake is eaten, it's gone. If you want more cake, you must go through the process of baking another one.

Let's say Jim decides to be tops in sales in his company. As his magnetic energy field connects him with what he needs to accomplish his goal, he is on a roll. Once he reaches his goal, his magnetic energy field related to that goal is dissolved. It is the same as turning off the oven once the cake is baked. There is nothing wrong with the oven. It simply needs to be turned on again. Likewise, there is nothing wrong with Jim. He simply needs to decide on a new goal, visualize himself already in possession of the end result, get the feeling of having it, and create a new magnetic energy field to help him reach his new goal.

Bigger-than-usual sales require a period of celebration followed by a period of rest. How long you celebrate and rest is entirely up to you. The next step is taking time to create your magnetic energy field for your next goal. Following these steps will prevent slumps after major accomplishments.

CHECKING FOR UNDERSTANDING

When There Is a Delay, Take Inventory

1. An I'm OK-You're OK attitude helps you solve problems.   T   F

2. When you come from the position of I'm not OK-You're OK, you want to get rid of people and things.   T   F

3. When your attitude is I'm OK-You're not OK, you don't have much patience with people.   T   F

4. An attitude of I'm not OK-You're not OK, keeps you cornered.   T   F

5. Dissolving accumulated energy has nothing to do with curing sales slumps.   T   F

6. By comparing yourself to others, then judging yourself, you may be blocking the achievement of your goal.   T   F

7. How you word your goal is not important, as long as you know what you mean.   T   F

8. Using your creative mind is just as important as using your logical mind in achieving your goals.   T   F

9. Feeling like you don't deserve to have something can be a block to your getting what you want.   T   F

10. Unresolved losses are painful, but have little effect on your losing things in your future.   T   F

Answers:

1. T	5. F	9. T
2. F	6. T	10. F
3. T	7. F	
4. T	8. T	

DISCOVERING LIMITING BELIEFS ABOUT YOUR PROFESSION

Directions: On a separate sheet of paper, make a list of the positive beliefs you have about your profession and the company for which you work or the company you own.

Example: It's great to be number one with the number one company.

Next make a list of the negative beliefs you have about your profession and the company for which you work (or the company you own).

Example: It's a dog-eat-dog business.

Directions: The following sentence beginnings will help you identify limiting ideas and conflicts about your goals. Complete them with whatever thoughts come to your mind.

1. "If I get this, I won't be able to _____."
2. "In order to do that, I'll have to give up _____."
3. "Once I _____ , I can no longer_____."
4. "You can't do that because_____."
5. "You can't make that much money unless_____."
6. "You can't have that kind of position in the company until _____."
7. "When you get to be _____ years old, you no longer can_____."
8. "Once you are _____ years old, your family no longer_____."
9. "With those injuries, you'll never be able to_____."
10. "With this many people out, we'll never be able to___."

Write positive denials followed by affirmations to dissolve these limiting beliefs from your subconscious.

MOVING FROM NEEDING TO HAVING

Directions: The first step in moving from needing to having is to identify your needs. On a separate sheet of paper, list needs that are important to you. Don't neglect writing things down because you don't have time to get those needs met now.

Examples:

- Time to learn a foreign language.
- Having your mate greet you at the door with a kiss.
- Being the top salesperson in your company.
- Being competent in some sport.
- Having a garden.
- Having your mate pay as much attention to you now as he or she did before the children arrived.

1. What have you always wanted that you've not yet let yourself have? Include clothes, vacations, awards, cars, houses, friends, ideal weight, time to read, the whole house straightened up at one time, increased profit of 40 percent and so on.

2. What compliments do you get that you don't fully accept or believe about yourself? After you have listed the compliments, find facts to support the truth of the compliments. This will help you fully accept the compliment. Be honest with yourself about how good you really are.

3. List the things you really do need (lack). Then write how you will get those needs satisfied.
   Do you need more sleep? Take a nap.
   Do you need to get the car cleaned up? Do it yourself or get it done.
   Do you need to take clothes to the cleaner? Do it or get it done.
   Do you need a massage? Get one.

> Do you need to do bookwork? Do it or get a secretary/ bookkeeper.
>
> Do you need to learn more closing techniques? Take a course.
>
> Do you need a more fulfilling relationship? List the aspects of a relationship that are important to you and communicate these to your mate.

While many of the items mentioned here may seem small, they weight heavily upon you when they pile up, and each clamors for attention. Be sure to visualize yourself with these needs satisfied. Remember, your subconscious doesn't need you to tell it how to produce the result. It just needs to know exactly what it is you want.

IDENTIFYING WHERE YOU SETTLE FOR LESS THAN YOU REALLY WANT

Directions: On a separate sheet of paper, list the general item you want. Next, list the specific characteristics that apply to that item. Then list any reason you can think of as to why you can't have exactly what you want in each item you choose. Once you have finished listing the reasons, write positive denial statements to erase these limiting ideas from your subconscious.

General	Specific	Reason
1. Car	1. Model, color, etc.	
2. House	2. Style, size, etc.	
3. College degree		
4. Clothes		
5. Sports		
6. Children		

Add your own.

IDENTIFYING PAST AND PRESENT FORMS OF PUNISHMENT

Directions: The following questions are offered to help you recall if you were punished as a child, and if so, what methods were used. On a separate sheet of paper, write down any punishments you received as a child.

1. As a child, were you deprived of fun as punishment? No TV, bike, recess?

2. Were you deprived of affection or attention? (Parenting person stopped talking to you for periods of time . . . you were sent to your room alone . . .)

3. Were you made to do some unpleasant task to "pay" for what you did? (Write sentences over and over, clean the garage, wash dishes for several nights, etc.)

4. List ways you were punished that were different from the above.

5. Take the examples of how you were punished and look for the general idea behind the punishment such as losing free time, paying money, being alone, losing the pleasure of your toys, etc.

Write positive denials and affirmations such as, "I no longer punish myself by taking things away from me when I make mistakes. I learn from my mistakes and correct them."

POSITIVE AFFIRMATIONS

Directions: Repeat these affirmations on a daily basis to internalize the principles of your subconscious and hasten the achievement of your desired results.

1. I word my goals correctly because my subconscious takes me literally.
2. I never compare myself to others and feel bad. I feel good about myself and rejoice in others' successes.
3. I believe I'm OK and others are OK too.
4. It's easy for me to relax and tap into my creativity.
5. I freely release all "loss energy" from my magnetic energy field.
6. If there is a delay in reaching my goal, I easily discover the cause and dissolve it.
7. I prevent slumps after major accomplishments by always programming ahead.

THE
SECRETS
OF
SUPERSELLING

Secret Ten

Dissolve Any Blocks and Refocus

PREVIEW OF SECRET TEN

DISSOLVE ANY BLOCKS AND REFOCUS

In Secret Ten you learn four levels of energy blocks that keep you from achieving your goals. You will also learn how negative magnetic energy fields repel from you the very goals you are trying to achieve and, most importantly, how to change them to positive magnetic energy fields.

DISSOLVE ANY BLOCKS AND REFOCUS

THE POWER OF ENERGY FIELDS

We've all heard the countless stories of people who say they are going to leave a mate who abuses them, yet stay; who vow they will never smoke again, yet continue to do so; who swear they'll never take another drink, but find themselves drinking again; or who continue in a job they hate even though they threaten to quit on a regular basis. Obviously there is something stronger than will power that causes people to repeat actions they really want to stop. That "something" is the negative magnetic energy field formed by your feelings and judgments about yourself and others based on previous traumatic experiences.

Before learning how to erase the negative magnetic energy field from your subconscious, let's examine two stories that illustrate just how powerful the negative programming can be. Both stories are startling examples of the power of your magnetic energy field and the role it plays in compulsive behavior.

Example: Childhood Experience Influences Career Choice

When Ann was eleven years old, her father was hospitalized with a medical condition. He then experienced a drug-induced psychosis. He became violent and had to be strapped in his hospital bed. At that time, the doctors did not have the medications to control psychotic behaviors that are available today.

Since Ann was loved so by her father, the doctor felt that seeing her might improve her father's condition, and he took Ann to her father's room. However, instead of calming down, Ann's father became even more agitated upon seeing her. He was verbally abusive and tried to attack her physically. Ann became so upset she developed an asthma attack, and had to be hospitalized herself.

Some time later, Ann's father recovered enough to return home. However, he was still a mentally sick man. He sat around polishing his guns and knives, talking of how he was going to kill himself and his family. These times were extremely frightening for Ann. Eventually, Ann's father was cured, and returned to his normal, fun-loving self. Following his recovery, Ann repressed all that had happened and gave no more thought to it.

Years later when it was time for a career choice, Ann decided to become a medical records administrator. While she did not enjoy this career, she was good at it, and went in and out of hospitals and nursing homes supervising medical records for twenty-nine years. Eventually, Ann moved 900 miles away and developed a new business in sales. Every two months, however, she would return to the hospitals and nursing homes where she was still retained as a consultant.

With her new career in sales, she often earned several thousand dollars in commissions for just a few hours' work. Yet she continued traveling 1,800 miles every two months to work for $100 to $300 a day. To top it off, she was traveling all that distance to do something she disliked doing. It didn't make much sense to Ann at the time, yet she felt powerless to stop going back.

During this time, Ann was doing some energy work with a therapist when she felt suddenly lighter and calmer. Her therapist explained that the light feeling she was experiencing was the result of released energy. This was "feeling" energy connected to the frightening times when her father had been ill.

As she released the energy, she experienced many of the same emotions she experienced during her father's illness. She relived the frightening time at the hospital, as well as the panic of going to sleep every night with a man in the house who was threatening to kill her. She felt relief as she let go of these stored-up emotions.

Two weeks later, Ann wrote letters of resignation to the hospitals and nursing homes she served. This was something she had fantasized doing many times before. Much to her delight, she found that her new career sky-rocketed from the increased positive energy she was able to focus on her selling.

Let's look now at some of the similarities between Ann's situation with her father and her career in medical records.

1. As a child, Ann was called into the hospital to help "cure" her father. In her career as a medical records consultant, she was not a member of the regular staff, but was called in as a consultant to help the nursing homes and hospitals do a more efficient job.

2. When she first went into the hospital, she found her father restrained in bed. While going in and out of nursing homes, she saw countless men and women restrained in beds and geriatric chairs. (Remember, that under stress, people cannot tell the difference between "objects." Therefore, to Ann, the patients in beds and chairs and her father were one and the same.)

3. There were similarities in roles as well. In going into the hospital to see her father, her role was to assist the staff in taking care of her father, the patient. In consulting with nursing homes, her role was to assist the staff in keeping the medical records in good order which eventually helped the patients.

4. In both situations, Ann maintained a certain level of distance. She did not actually deal with her father other than talking to him. Likewise, in the hospitals and nursing homes, she did not deal with the patients other than talking to them in passing.

Prior to releasing the emotional energy stuck in her negative magnetic energy field, Ann would be comforted by being able to go into the nursing homes and hospitals and to leave unharmed. On an unconscious level, she was reassured that Daddy was restrained and couldn't hurt her. Once the negative energy was released, she no longer needed this reassurance.

Example: Seeking Father's Approval Richard was a very creative young man who was full of ideas about how to do things better. He had a strong desire to be an entrepreneur, and he frequently went to his father with ideas about starting businesses. Sometimes he went just to get his father's support and approval. Other times he needed venture capital, and his father was a necessary link in getting the needed money.

Richard's father always shot down his ideas, and refused to help him financially with his ventures. Richard saw his father as an authority figure who controlled the purse strings, and never valued his ideas.

This pattern established by Richard and his father was repeated over and over throughout Richard's life. He attended college and received a teaching degree. At the school where he taught, he began sharing his ideas about how things could be improved. His principal, whom he saw as an authority or father figure, said that his ideas were great and that he'd pass them on to the board. However, Richard never received any feedback about his ideas. In another school, the principal always said, "No, we can't do that. It won't work, and besides we don't have the funding." Because of these and similar experiences, Richard left education for business. In business, he found himself working for employers who told him his ideas were no good and/or there wasn't enough money to do them. These experiences were repeated again and again, following the same old pattern.

After years of frustration, Richard decided to seek help. While working through various blocks to success, he began to see the similarity between the authority figures that seemed to control his life and his father. He eventually dissolved the need to seek his father's and other authority figures' approval of his ideas. Once this negative energy was dissolved from his magnetic energy field, he went on to form his own successful ventures.

When there is a situation in your life that is highly charged with emotion, it can become stuck in your energy field. Once stuck, it continues to vibrate at that frequency, and causes you to think, feel, and act the same way again and again. It's like tuning your radio to your favorite station. You don't get classical music one day, and country the next. You get the same kind of music over and over. The songs may have different titles, but the basic style of music is the same.

While Ann's story is a little unusual, Richard's experience is very common. Both stories illustrate the point that once an experience becomes stuck in your magnetic energy field, it gets repeated over and over until the pattern in which it is formed is dissolved.

DON'T TRY TO FIGURE IT OUT . . . DISSOLVE IT

Unwanted programming is detrimental to the achievement of your goals in your professional life. However, trying to figure out *why* you did what you did, or *why* you have a block to achieving your sales goal is often a waste of time. Let's compare dissolving sales blocks to sweetening a glass of iced tea.

Let's say you have a glass of unsweetened, iced tea and several sugar cubes. If you have ever tried to get sugar cubes to dissolve in cold tea, you know how difficult it is.

While you are having difficulty getting the sugar cubes dissolved, would you spend time wondering how the sugar got formed into cubes in the first place? Would you try to determine how much the machines cost that cut each cube just the right size, or why they even decided to make sugar in the form of cubes? Probably not. Even if you came up with the answers to these questions, none of the information would help you reach your goal of quickly sweetening your tea.

However, if you focused your attention on sweetening the tea, (rather than trying to figure out how and why the sugar cubes got that way), you might remember that you can pour boiling water over sugar cubes and get a simple syrup. This syrup would easily sweeten your tea. The point we're making is that when you are faced with an obstacle or block, your time can best be used in identifying that obstacle and then dissolving it, rather than puzzling over *why* you have the obstacle.

Likewise, if you have had unsatisfactory experiences in your sales career, it is not necessary to figure out what went wrong in each case, and understand why you acted the way you did. Instead of trying to figure it out, dissolve it. The following example illustrates this point.

Example: Fear of Closing
Martha was a salesperson who always seemed to come up short

when it came to closing her sales. Her presentations always seemed to go well, but for some reason, she couldn't get her customers to sign on the dotted line. As she reviewed her presentations, she realized that she often neglected to ask for a definite decision. By not asking for the decision, she avoided the possibility of getting a "no." She almost always waited for the prospect to say, "I want to buy this!" She realized that not asking for the decision was a habit not only in her professional life, but in her personal life as well.

At this point she could have spent a lot of time unraveling the mystery of why she dreaded asking people to make a decision. She might have remembered times when she had asked her parents to allow her to do something of importance, and they said, "No." She might have discovered times when she had asked someone she worked for to make a decision important to her career, and they said, "No." But even if she had pinpointed exactly why she developed the fear of asking for decisions, it would not have dissolved the problem. It actually could have reinforced the fear by giving her a reason for having it. You have probably known people who told you they couldn't do a certain thing, such as climbing a ladder, because of a childhood trauma of falling off a swing, falling out of a tree or falling down a high flight of stairs.

Fortunately, Martha decided to dissolve her fear of closing rather than to look for the experiences that led to her developing the fear. She began by replacing the idea that she wasn't a good closer with the image of herself as a great closer. She pictured herself asking the customer to buy and the customer enthusiastically buying. She quit telling people she was poor at closing. She made tangible pictures of herself and customers and scripted them with, "This is me closing sale after sale."

Once Martha dissolved her fear of closing and accepted the idea of being a good closer, her sales increased dramatically.

Once you've reprogrammed your thoughts, your subconscious *must* determine how to produce the result you have chosen. As you accept the idea of being a great closer or prospector, you start behaving differently. You may find a book that is helpful in this area. Perhaps a friend tells you about a workshop that teaches you new sales techniques. The possibilities of how you achieve your goal are endless.

Clearing Out the Old Is Crucial

You simply can't put a new car in a one-car garage if the old car is still there. Just as you must remove the old car to make room for the new, you must dissolve the negative energy attached to situations that are not the way you want them to be.

As long as an idea exists in your subconscious, you will have the situation that matches that idea in your life. By changing the idea, you change the result. By dissolving the idea, you no longer have that result.

You can dissolve ideas and energy from your subconscious by using positive denials, affirmations, visualization processes, and forgiveness processes. As you dissolve the old energy patterns, you no longer experience those negative situations. You'll learn more about how to do this in the next section.

DISSOLVING NEGATIVE ENERGY

Level One Energy Blocks

Sometimes dissolving negative energy is accomplished by simply experiencing some negative feelings related to things currently happening in your life. These feelings have been temporarily blocked from your conscious awareness, and doing one or more of the following activities will help you get in touch with them. As you release this built-up energy, you simply refocus it in a positive direction.

As you do the following activities, allow yourself to experience your emotions without judging yourself or anyone else. Don't try to figure out why you feel like you do. Don't try to think about fixing any problems that might have been caused as a result of what happened. Simply feel your emotions with the idea of letting the negative energy change into positive energy. There is no set amount of time that is needed for this to happen. It can happen in minutes, or it may take hours.

Activities to Dissolve Level One Energy Blocks

1. This list of activities is an excellent way to physically dissolve level one energy blocks. Choose whichever activities appeal to you and do them in a place where it is okay to make noise, and where you will not be interrupted.

   a. Pound a pillow. (Be sure pillow is full enough to protect your hand.)

   b. Pound a board with a hammer.

   c. Roll up a towel, and hit a solid object with it.

   d. Throw empty bottles in a trash can hard enough to break them.

   e. Have a temper tantrum on your bed. Scream, yell, really let go.

   f. Hit a tennis ball repeatedly against a wall.

   As you do any of the activities suggested above, you may suddenly experience feelings that have been blocked from your conscious awareness. Remember, you don't have to do anything about them. Just experience your feelings fully. By doing so, you will allow them to be released and transformed into positive energy.

2. Another powerful way to clear unwanted energy patterns or blocks is through the use of visualization. Visualization is the process of seeing and experiencing events in your imagination as if you were experiencing them in real life. The only limits on what you are able to visualize are the limits which you place on your own imagination.

   When doing the visualization process, find a place where you will have absolute quiet. Unplug the telephone. If you live with other people, make sure you will not be interrupted, then do the following steps:

   a. Begin by relaxing your body and mind. Try a warm bath, play some soothing music, etc.

   b. Once you are relaxed, close your eyes and imagine a TV set in front of you. On the set you see the situation you want to change. Next, bring someone into the scene whom you admire. See and hear this person tell you it is okay for you to change the way things are in your life.

c. Now imagine you have a miner's cap on your head. Focus the light on the cap so it is illuminating the scene on the TV set. As the light bathes everyone in the scene, think of it as unconditional, positive energy which dissolves all negative feelings, just as boiling water dissolves ice. Continue to focus the light until you experience a peaceful, happy feeling about the situation.

d. Now change things around in the scene so that everyone and everything is just the way you want it to be. If you have been giving up after your prospect's first no, imagine yourself closing two, three, four, five times. If you've been comparing yourself to others and feeling bad because your production is lower than theirs, imagine yourself receiving the same production awards they receive.

e. Experience the positive feelings associated with this scene with as much intensity as you possibly can. Hold the new picture for at least half a minute.

f. Now let go of this picture by changing the channel on the TV so that you see a blank screen. Stop consciously thinking about things. Be calm, and ready to let your subconscious tell you what to do, where to go, whom to call, and so on. Listen to the creative spark within you. The answer may not come immediately. You may feel sleepy, because this is the way the creative brain sometimes works. If so, take a short nap, and have pen and paper ready so you can record any ideas that come to you as you awaken. (Creative people frequently take naps when faced with challenges.)

g. Continue visualizing daily until you achieve the result(s) you want. See the same scene each time, keeping all the details the same.

Level Two Energy Blocks

If it is easy for you to experience your feelings, doing the activities suggested in level one energy blocks will be enough. Once you have fully experienced your feelings, you can go on to achieving your goals. However, unwanted energy patterns may have accumulated in your energy field that you are unable to dissolve with level one activities.

There are a number of possible reasons for this: You may have built thick walls around your emotions to protect yourself from painful feelings. You may have denied your feelings in order to be polite or to protect yourself from hurting people's feelings or making them angry. You may believe you have fully dealt with your feelings because you have talked about them to someone else. Talking about being mad and really feeling your anger are two different experiences. Dealing with the mental level is necessary, but the job is not complete until your feelings are fully experienced, thereby dissolving that energy pattern from your energy field.

Activities to Dissolve Level Two Energy Blocks

When your feelings are blocked on this deeper level as described above, it is called a level two energy block. The first step in clearing this is to program your subconscious to allow you to be *consciously* aware of your thoughts and feelings. You can do this by reading the following statements out loud each day for at least a week (longer if necessary).

1. "I allow myself to experience my thoughts and feelings about_____."
Fill in the blank with the person's name or the situation.

Example: "I allow myself to experience my thoughts and feelings about closing (prospecting, interest rates changing, etc.)."

Once you know what your feelings are, you work with the following statements.

1. "I no longer feel _____ (angry, sad, scared) about_____."

2. "I no longer judge myself for thinking and feeling the way I have in the past about_____."

Example: "I no longer feel scared about asking for a buying decision. I no longer judge myself for being scared in the past about closing."

In addition to the general statements in numbers one and two, you must write specific positive denials and affirmations regarding your own situation. To help you identify the needed positive denials and affirmations, do the following:

1. Use the John James game plan as presented in Secret Nine to jot down in as few words as possible what has been happening. For example, "I came into the job thinking I was going to do really well very fast. I'm used to being one of the best at what I do. That hasn't happened. I feel discouraged, and I wonder if I'm in the wrong business."

2. To make it easier to discover your negative judgments and feelings, pretend the situation happened to someone else, and ask yourself, "What might someone be thinking and feeling in that situation?" For example, a person might make a judgment like, "I am only an average producer in this business." There could be a feeling of sadness, anger, fear, or a combination of all three.

3. Continue by asking yourself, "What critical opinions might someone have about that? What comparisons might the person be making about himself and others?" For example, "I'm not as good at sales as John, Sam, and Jane. I'll never be able to make ends meet with this job!"

Once you are aware of your negative and limiting judgments, write positive denials and affirmations to erase them from your energy field.

Examples:

- "I no longer feel mad about not having closed well in the past. I now feel happy and proud that I close well."
- "I don't feel discouraged and wonder if I'm in the wrong business anymore. I'm excited about my career in sales."

- "It's not true that I won't be able to make ends meet with this job. Not only will I make ends meet, I will have money left over to use for fun, to save, and to invest."

Read the denials and affirmations on a daily basis (or make and play your personal tape of the positive denials and affirmations). Once again, there is no set amount of times you will need to repeat these statements. A few times may be enough, or it may take many repetitions. Allow yourself to experience your feelings as they surface, and repeat the activities suggested for dissolving level one energy blocks.

Level Three Energy Blocks

You may do all the activities suggested in levels one and two, and still be unable to dissolve the negative energy that is blocking your goal achievement. If so, the problem may be that while you are aware of your thoughts and feelings, you are unable to forgive yourself and others for what happened. This is called a level three energy block. The next crucial step in clearing your energy field is to forgive yourself and others for any mistakes or offenses.

The purpose of forgiveness
is to free yourself from the negative
experience so that it doesn't get repeated
in your life.

Sometimes people react negatively to the idea of forgiveness because of the feelings they have as they think about the word. If this is true for you, try to set that aside as you look at the dictionary's definition of forgiveness.

To Forgive:

- To excuse for a fault or an offense.
- To renounce anger or resentment against.
- To absolve from payment of.
- To pass over an offense without demanding punishment.
- To free the offender from the consequences of the offense.
- To grant pardon without harboring resentment.

***Forgiveness can be summarized as the absence
of negative feelings about yourself and others,
no matter what has happened.***

How Does Being Unwilling to Forgive Hurt You?

Let's look more closely at what happens on an energy level when
you are angry at someone.

(You) ⌒⌒⌒⌒⌒ ➡ ⌒⌒⌒⌒⌒ (person at whom
you are angry)

If the person you have negative feelings about has no negative
feelings about you or the situation you're angry about, your
negative energy cannot affect him or her. It is impossible for that
person to receive the negative feelings, just as it is impossible for
you to personally receive a package from the post office when you
are not at home.

⌒⌒⌒⌒⌒⌒ ➡ ⌒⌒⌒⌒⌒⌒⌒⌒⌒⌒⌒⌒⌒⌒ ☐

As you see in the diagram, the offender is missing from the
picture. When a person has no negative energy about himself or
a given situation, his energy field is vibrating at a different
frequency than the person who is angry with him. This removes
him from the picture.

⌒⌒⌒⌒⌒ ➡ ⌒⌒⌒⌒⌒⌒⌒⌒⌒⌒⌒⌒⌒⌒⌒⌒⌒⌒ ⬇

⬆ ⌒⌒⌒⌒⌒⌒⌒⌒⌒⌒⌒⌒⌒⌒⌒⌒⌒⌒⌒⌒⌒⌒⌒ ⬅

The negative energy you send passes right by him or her, and
returns to you, because energy flows in a circuit. In addition,
what you focus on expands and increases, so you get more
negative energy back than you sent out.

(You) ⌒⌒⌒⌒⌒➡⌒⌒⌒⌒⌒⌒➡ (person at whom you
are angry)

(You)⬅⌒⌒⌒⌒⌒⌒⌒⌒⌒⌒⌒⌒⌒⌒⌒⌒⌒⌒⬅

If the person you have negative feelings about also has
negative feelings about you or the situation, he or she receives
your energy and becomes even angrier than before. This increased energy is returned to you.

If you are the person against whom an offense has been committed, and you are holding on to your negative feelings about it, there is no way you can escape feeling worse and worse. You are caught in a no-win situation. If the offender accepts your negative feelings and sends them back to you, you receive an increased amount of negative feelings. If the offender doesn't accept your negative feelings, they still come back to you multiplied.

To free yourself from negative energy, stop punishing yourself and others for mistakes and offenses. However, even though you have decided not to punish, you may still *want* to punish. You know you still have the desire to punish when you think thoughts like, "Well, I'm not going to do it, but I'd sure like to call all their customers and tell them how irresponsibly that company conducts business." To be free, you must also give up the desire to punish along with the feeling of triumph you get when you pay someone back for a wrong they did to you.

***To forgive means to let go of the judgments
and feelings you have about what has happened.***

Identifying the People and Situations Connected to Level Three Energy Blocks

Sometimes you may hold on to negative feelings and thoughts without being aware of doing so. When working with level three energy blocks, it is necessary to let go of bitterness and anger about the offense as well as the person committing the offense. For example, you may have excused your son who wrecked your car and still be holding bitterness about the situation of the car being wrecked. You may have pardoned yourself for misjudging an employee whom you thought had great promise, and yet still be resentful about the situation of the employee turning out to be mediocre. You may have forgiven a customer for backing out of a big deal, but still feel disappointed about the deal falling through. Be sure that you deal with your feelings about the offense or situation as well as your feelings about the person responsible for the offense. To discover if you are harboring any bitterness or anger, take some time to consider the following:

1. Make a list of people you need to forgive for things they have done to you.
2. Make a list of people from whom you want forgiveness for things you have done to them.
3. Make a list of situations and offenses about which you still have negative feelings (fear, anger, disappointment, sadness, guilt).

Examples:

- Stock market drops excessively.
- Car gets wrecked.
- Not doing as well as others.
- Interest rates go up.
- Failure to reach sales quota.

Activities to Dissolve Level Three Energy Blocks When Someone Has Wronged You

1. Find a quiet place where you can be alone and will not be interrupted.
2. Quiet your mind and body. Imagine there is a TV set in front of you. On the TV set see a picture of someone who has wronged you. Say to that person, "I now let go of my anger, my bitterness, and my hurt feelings about you and what you did. I no longer want to pay you back, or want you to hurt as I have been hurting. You are forgiven."
3. Take the list of wrong-doings others have done to you. Mentally form the list to look like a sugar cube. Imagine a teapot full of boiling water. Hear the whistling sound it makes when the water is boiling. See the boiling water poured over the sugar cube of resentments, sadness, loss, desire for revenge, and so forth. Watch as the sugar cube of wrong-doings others have done to you dissolves, and feel the upset feelings leave your body. As this happens, a positive feeling settles over you, bringing with it a sense of peace.

When You Have Wronged Someone

1. Find a quiet place where you can be alone and will not be interrupted.

2. Relax your mind and body. Imagine there is a TV set in front of you. On it is a picture of someone you have wronged. Say, "I ask you to let go of your angry, hurt feelings about me and what I did to you. Please stop wanting to pay me back, or wanting me to hurt as you have. I now dissolve any thoughts and feelings of guilt about what I have done to you. I no longer want to punish myself for what I have done to you. I am forgiven. I am free."

3. Take the list of wrong-doings you have done to others. Mentally form the list to look like a sugar cube. Imagine a teapot full of boiling water. Hear the whistling sound it makes when the water is boiling. See the boiling water poured over the sugar cube of guilt, resentments, sadness, loss, desire for revenge, fear, and so forth. Watch as the sugar cube of wrong-doings you have done to others dissolves, and feel the upset feelings leave your body. As this happens, a positive feeling settles over you, bringing with it a sense of peace.

Situations About Which You Still Have Negative Feelings

1. Find a quiet place where you can be alone and will not be interrupted.

2. Relax your mind and body. Imagine there is a TV set in front of you. On it is a picture of a situation about which you are still angry, fearful, disappointed, sad, or feeling guilty. Say, "I now let go of my feelings of guilt, anger, etc. about what happened. I no longer feel bad about it, and this won't happen again."

3. Take the list of situations about which you have negative feelings. Mentally form the list to look like a sugar cube. Imagine a teapot full of boiling water. Hear the whistling

sound it makes when the water is boiling. See the boiling water poured over the sugar cube of guilt, resentments, sadness, loss, fear, and so forth. Watch as the sugar cube of situations dissolves, and feel the upset feelings leave your body. As this happens, a positive feeling settles over you, bringing with it a sense of peace.

Level Four Energy Blocks

When you have done the suggested activities in levels one, two and three and still have not reached your goal, you may be dealing with a level four energy block.

If you are stuck at this level, you probably have been faithful in carrying out the activities suggested by your company. You put in long hours. You have done all the appropriate activities to reach your sales goals. You have followed all the training suggestions. You may also have followed the suggestions put forth in this book.

You know there is a block somewhere, but you have been unable to identify it. You still are not achieving to the level you desire, and know is possible.

The root cause of a level four block is a negative denial system that not only prevents you from achieving your goal, but may also keep you from discovering the cause of your block. At the base of this negative denial system are judgments.

JUDGMENTS MAY BE KEPT FROM YOUR CONSCIOUS MIND THROUGH DENIAL

Judgments may be made on a feeling level without your being consciously aware of them, and kept from your conscious mind through the process of Denial. When in a state of denial, you may refuse to grant your own requests, or acknowledge your feelings. (This is covered in detail in Secret Four.)

In a level four energy block, there is an accumulation of times when you have run up against the roadblock of one of your ego states absolutely refusing to agree to go along with what you want or worse yet, refusing to even listen to your request. Negative denials are held in place in your magnetic energy field with judgments, emotional control, and suppression of feelings.

The combination of negative denials and judgments together prevent you from dissolving unwanted energy patterns. As you refuse to acknowledge your judgments and feelings, you are trapped in the patterns created by the judgments.

However, it is possible to clear the accumulated energy by doing the following:

1. Believe that this block can be dissolved.
2. Set a goal to dissolve all the negative energy connected to these experiences as quickly and easily as possible.
3. Make a decision to grant your own requests *now* in spite of previous refusals.

Activities to Dissolve Level Four Energy Blocks

1. Do the suggested activities in levels one, two and three.
2. In addition to the specific positive denials and affirmations you have already identified, declare the following:

- "It's not true that I don't deserve the things I want."
- "It's not true that I don't deserve to keep what I get."
- "I'm not bad. Nobody takes anything away from me anymore."
- "Nobody keeps me from getting what I want. I am reaching my goal, I am keeping it when I get it, and I never feel bad after I feel good anymore!"
- "I dissolve all previously accepted limits on how much I deserve to have, be, or do. Nature's way is abundance. Since I am a part of Nature, I have an abundance of all good things."

Identifying your own personal denials is crucial in dissolving the judgments and freeing your energy to create new results. Once you have identified them, say your statements daily with as much intensity as you can create. It is necessary that you say them out loud (or play your own tape) until you reach your goals.

3. Recall people who are now living who have an abundance of friends, health, money, power, and achievements. Think of people who have done well in your chosen field. Once you have a clear picture of the people you respect and admire, imagine them rolling out the red carpet for you and inviting you to join them. See yourself being welcomed into their midst. Feel their love and acceptance, and your gratitude. Hear someone in the crowd whom you respect declaring in a loud voice, "From this day forward, _____ (say your name here) will never again feel unworthy of being a full-fledged member of this group in good standing."

   See people coming up to shake your hand, and hear them congratulating you. Enjoy celebrating this happy occasion. (Repeat this visualization daily until you have achieved the specific results you're working on. Thereafter, it is a good idea to repeat the process weekly or at least monthly.)

4. Put photographs of the people you identified earlier on a piece of paper. Put your picture in the center so you are surrounded by them. At the bottom of the picture, write "I'm included. I belong." Look at the picture daily.

As you clear Negative Denials and Judgments from your emotional, mental, and physical energy, your subconscious can produce results for you according to the new patterns you create.

CHECKING FOR UNDERSTANDING

Dissolve Any Blocks and Refocus

1. When you don't dissolve your negative feelings about situations, you get more of the same situations.   T   F

2. Before you can dissolve energy patterns, you must first figure out how things got to be the way they are.   T   F

3. Using your intuition and creativity to solve problems and reach goals is the same as trying to figure out what to do. T F

4. As you repeatedly try to figure out why you're in a slump and not selling, you are unknowingly creating the goal of not selling. T F

5. Dissolving negative energy doesn't have anything to do with curing sales slumps. T F

6. Judgments mold your energy into a pattern and keep it that way as long as the judgments last. T F

7. Judgments and feelings only affect your results when you are conscious of them. T F

8. Judgments go hand-in-hand with denials to keep your energy formed in a certain pattern. T F

9. Denials are held in place with judgments and the control or suppression of feelings. T F

10. You don't have to clear up unwanted energy patterns; just concentrating on skill training alone will solve the problem of not reaching goals. T F

11. Unconditional forgiveness energy has more power than fear, anger, resentment, etc. T F

12. Giving up anger and hurt, etc. about an offense is just as important as excusing the offender. T F

13. Dissolving the image and idea from your subconscious means you no longer have that result in your life. T F

14. Judgments are simply idle thoughts. T F

15. Writing positive denials and affirmations erases unwanted thoughts from your subconscious. T F

16. A positive denial is one that refuses to   T   F
    acknowledge that something is true.

Answers:

1. T	6. T	11. T
2. F	7. F	12. T
3. F	8. T	13. T
4. T	9. T	14. F
5. F	10. F	15. T
		16. T

CHECKLIST FOR SUCCESS

Use this checklist as a guide to make sure you have covered all the steps necessary to attain your goal(s). It can also be used to discover blocks that are keeping you from getting the result(s) you want.

	Yes	No

1. Have you been specific about your goal, including small details?

2. Have you checked the wording of your goal?

3. Do you have a strong desire for this result?

4. Do you believe you can achieve this result?

5. Are you willing to let yourself have what you want?

6. Have you decided on an end result?

7. Have you made a tangible representation of your end result?

8. Are you visualizing the end result daily?

9. Do you have a feeling of "having" your goal rather than "needing" it?

10. Are you relaxed and confident as you think about your goal?

	Yes	No

11. Have you taken a block of uninterrupted time to create your positive magnetic energy field?

12. Are you visualizing your energy radiating out in the form of your goal?

13. Are you visualizing your energy returning to you in the form of your goal?

14. Have you identified limiting judgments related to your goal?

15. Have you written positive denials and affirmations to dissolve them?

16. Have you identified limiting beliefs related to your goal?

17. Have you written positive denials and affirmations to dissolve them?

18. Have you identified fears related to your goal?

19. Have you written positive denials and affirmations to dissolve them?

20. Have you identified wrongdoings you've done and those others have done to you?

21. Have you cleared up wrongdoings?

22. Have you dissolved negative feelings from past experiences?

23. Have you expanded your self image to include your goal?

24. Have you identified celebrations that are meaningful to you?

25. Are you celebrating your accomplishments on a regular basis?

26. Are you remembering to set new goals after major accomplishments, thereby avoiding "dry spells?"

Ideally you will answer yes to each question.

> *If you have gotten off track, do what is needed*
> *so that you can answer each question with*
> *a "yes." This helps you refocus your attention*
> *on the positive achievement of your*
> *desired result.*

POSITIVE AFFIRMATIONS

Directions: Repeat these affirmations on a daily basis to internalize the principles of your subconscious, and hasten the achievement of your desired results.

1. I'm so grateful that I don't judge or punish myself for mistakes I made in the past. I unconditionally forgive myself and others.

2. It's not true that I don't deserve what I want or deserve to keep what I get. I am fully deserving of all my goals.

3. Nobody takes anything away from me that is rightfully mine.

4. I dissolve all previously accepted limits on how much I deserve to have, be, or do. I am free to achieve to whatever level I choose.

AND NOW WHAT?

Now that you have read *The Secrets of SuperSelling*, we suggest that you review the Dream List you wrote when you started this book. How many things have you already accomplished? How many things have you thought of but not yet added to your list? What would you do if you were sure there was no possibility of failure? What projects would you tackle if you had unlimited financial resources? What places would you visit if you had the time and money to do so? What exciting endeavor would you be involved in if you knew you could sell your ideas to powerful people?

Imagine that it is ten years from now. Where are you living and working? What is your net worth? What special contributions have you made to yourself, your family, and the planet? Describe your ideal life in as few words as possible. Your picture may be very different from your present reality. Don't let fear jump in and tell you that it is impossible to make that ideal picture real.

Walt Disney once said, "Somehow I can't believe there are many heights that can't be scaled by a man who knows the secret to making dreams come true. This special secret can be summarized in four C's. They are: curiosity, confidence, courage, and constancy, and the greatest of these is confidence."

It is our belief that knowing how to control the most powerful, creative instrument in the universe, your subconscious, gives you the confidence to tackle any dream you may have. You now know the Secrets. However, knowing them without applying them on a daily basis is like having a banquet set before you and never testing a delicious mouthful. The application of the information is up to you. You must do it for yourself.

If you are hesitant to tackle your dreams because it would take so long to achieve them, remember that you can create your own reality. Your ideal life may not be as far away as you presently think. How long do you think it would take an insurance agency to go from twenty-ninth nationally to sixth? Charlie Garrison of The Farmers Insurance Group in California made that jump in just eight months. Don't buy into other people's reality about how long it takes to accomplish goals or how hard it is to do so. Set your own time frames and keep track of what is happening. If you don't reach your goal in the time set, take inventory of your subconscious, dissolve limiting ideas and set a new time frame. Applying the Secrets as a way of life is going to take some work, some time, some effort and a definite commitment to enhancing the quality of your life. The rewards, however, are well worth the investment.

As we said earlier, our mutual mission is to help you gain control of your subconscious so that you make more sales, earn more money, and have more fun doing it! *The Secrets of Super-Selling* has been designed for learning, not entertainment. The fun comes from achieving the results you create through applying the principles. The Secrets you have learned can be applied to every area of your life. They can be used to increase your business, enhance the quality of your relationships, improve your health, improve your golf score, and more! It is our sincere hope that you internalize the Secrets to the degree that you just naturally use them in your everyday life.

We encourage you to write and share your success stories with us. Please contact us if we may be of service to you in any of the following ways:

- Add you to our mailing list
- Conduct a Secrets workshop in your area
- Consult with you or your company

Life Skills Unlimited
Carl Stevens & Associates
P.O.Box 627
Imperial Beach, CA 91933

BIBLIOGRAPHY

Andersen, Uell S. *Three Magic Words*. Hollywood, California: Wilshire Book Company, 1979.

Barnes, Graham. *Transactional Analysis After Eric Berne*. New York: Harper & Row, 1977.

Blakeslee, Thomas R. *The Right Brain*. New York: Doubleday, 1980.

Fairbairn, William. *An Object Relations Theory of the Personality*. New York: Basic Books, 1952.

Harris, Thomas A. *I'm OK—You're OK*. New York: Avon, 1969.

Hendricks, G. & Willis, R. *The Centering Book*. Englewood Cliffs, New Jersey: Prentice Hall, 1977.

Herbert, Nick. *Quantum Reality—Beyond the New Physics*. New York: Doubleday, 1985.

Hill, Napoleon. *Think & Grow Rich*. Hollywood, California: Wilshire Book Co., 1966.

Holmes, Ernest. *Creative Mind And Success*. New York: Dodd, Mead & Company, 1957.

Journal of Creative Behavior, 10(A): 239–49, "Putting Our Whole Brain to Use," Susan V. Garrett, "A Fresh Look at the Creative Process," 1976.

Koestler, A. *The Act of Creation*. New York: Dell Publishing Co., 1975.

Maltz, Maxwell. *Psycho-Cybernetics*. New York: Prentice Hall, 1960

Nebes, Robert D. *The Human Brain*. New Jersey: Prentice-Hall, 1977.

Omstein, Robert. *The Psychology of Consciousness*. California: W.H. Freeman & Co., 1972.

Penfield, Wilder. *The Mystery of the Mind*. Princeton: Princeton Univ. Press, 1975.

Russell, Peter. *The Brain Book*. New York: E.P. Dutton, Inc., 1979.

Shapiro, Deane, *Meditation: Classic and Contemporary Perspectives*. Hawthorne, New York, Aldine Publishing Company, 1984.

Tart, C. *States of Consciousness*. New York: E.P. Dutton, 1975.